top 50 INDOOR PLANTS

and how **NOT** *to kill them!*

ANGIE THOMAS

HarperCollins*Publishers*

CONTENTS

INTRODUCTION

Gardening is a fabulous way to connect with nature and improve your health and wellbeing. Research has shown that gardening can have a positive effect on life satisfaction, your sense of community and quality of life, in addition to helping reduce depression, anxiety and even body mass index.

Whether you're lucky enough to have a big backyard with a flourishing flower and vegetable garden, or you have the tiniest studio apartment, indoor plants give you the opportunity to bring the outdoors in and have a garden, no matter what type and size of space you have. There's an indoor plant for almost every spot!

Indoor plants have gone through several different interior design phases in recent decades. In the 1970s and 1980s, you might have seen a single palm or rubber plant tucked away in the corner of a living room, a fern in a macramé hanger in the kitchen and an African violet on a windowsill.

The 1990s featured restrained, low key design, and indoor plants went missing from many households. Their disappearance may have also had something to do with people not knowing how to care for indoor plants and a fear of killing yet another poor specimen.

Thankfully, there has been a massive revival of interest in indoor plants and their popularity has skyrocketed. The reasons for this could include people's desire to be more connected with nature in increasingly green-space deprived and crowded cities and suburbs, the immense pleasure and satisfaction that can be derived from watching an indoor plant grow and flourish, and that nurturing plants is a wonderfully slow and relaxing pastime – a perfect antidote for the frantic pace of modern life.

Whatever the reasons for our increasing desire to include more greenery in our lives, this heightened interest has been matched by garden centres stocking a larger number and variety of indoor plants and a boom in specialist indoor plant growers as well as passionate private collectors. To satisfy the public's demand for all things indoor plants, huge ticket-entry sales events are being held in warehouses, and online plant stores are continually sold out of the hottest items. There are multiple social media sites, with tens or hundreds of thousands of followers, dedicated solely to growing indoor plants. Our hunger for indoor plants with new and interesting traits, or that are easier to grow and maintain, is keeping plant breeders busy. New and improved ways of growing plants indoors, such as in vertical gardens, means we can grow plants in previously unused places around our homes. Fantastic interior spaces can now be designed with plants in mind, rather than plants being an afterthought.

When you team our renewed fascination for indoor plants with beautiful designer pots and plant stands, and the trend for recycling household objects into planters or making your own from scratch (including a revival in macramé hanging basket holders!), the indoor plant revolution is becoming a powerful force that will hopefully continue to fill our homes with greenery well into the future.

Beyond the aesthetic and lifestyle reasons for growing plants, over recent decades there has been an increasing amount of research done regarding the health benefits of growing plants indoors. This has been prompted by the realisation that the air inside our homes, offices, schools and buildings can be more polluted than the air outside. Furniture, carpets, gas cooking and heating, paint and household cleaning products can all contribute to indoor air pollution and adversely affect our health.

NASA conducted a 'Clean Air Study' that examined the levels of various toxic chemicals in the air that could be reduced by plants. They looked at chemicals such as benzene, xylene, toluene and formaldehyde, which are found in plastics and furniture, and ammonia, which is a common ingredient in cleaning products. Plants can absorb and process these chemicals, making them harmless, or simply soak them up and remove them from indoor air. The study found that different plants had varying abilities to filter toxins from the air, with plants like the humble peace lily and mother-in-law's tongue being particularly effective at this. The greater the number of plants, the better the potential air purifying benefits. The microbes found in potting mix may also play an important part in filtering the air.

Plant Life Balance, a not-for-profit horticulture R&D organisation, together with RMIT University and the University of Melbourne, calculated that just one medium sized indoor plant in a room of 20 square metres (20m^2) can lead to 25% cleaner air, increasing to 75% with 5 plants, and 10 plants providing the maximum level of clean air benefits.

Plant Life Balance also studied the psychological effects of indoor plants and found that 'a few plants can make you feel more relaxed, inspired and positive', with 5 medium sized plants in a 20m^2 room providing a 60% improvement in wellbeing. The more variety in plant types the better, and 10 plants in a 20m^2 space will give you the maximum benefit.

Companies are also recognising the benefits of indoor plants and introducing them into their offices, with green walls and large potted displays now featuring in many buildings; personal office desk plants are also becoming wonderfully common. Research conducted by the University of Technology, Sydney, showed that indoor plants not only improve air quality in office environments, they also help to reduce sick leave, stress and negativity, and boost people's performance, productivity and job satisfaction. That's a pretty impressive resume!

Preliminary research has also shown that by growing plants in school classrooms, performance in spelling, maths, science and reading can be improved, particularly where students have limited access to gardening and nature based activities.

All these amazing benefits just from growing indoor plants!

Whether you've always wanted to try growing an indoor plant and never had the courage, have tried in the past and not been particularly successful, or would like to expand your current collection of indoor plants, this book will help you to work out what plants you can grow in different indoor spaces and how to care for them. Welcome to the wonderful world of indoor plants!

WHAT TO GROW WHERE

A very important part of successfully growing indoor plants is to find the right spot for them. A sun-loving plant will not thrive in a dimly lit corner, and a humid bathroom can be a recipe for disaster for a plant that prefers a well ventilated, airy spot. Have a look around your home and think about the areas you would like to 'greenify'. Take note of:

- The level of light and how that changes throughout the day and across the seasons
- Does the room get particularly hot or cold at different times of the year?
- Is it draughty or exposed to air conditioning or heating?
- The level of humidity
- What horizontal and vertical spaces are available

Once you know the details of the where, then think about what foliage shapes, styles and colours tickle your fancy. Are you keen on green, lush and jungle-esque? Or perhaps you're a sucker for succulents? Then it's simply a matter of matching the where with the what.

In the following pages you'll discover what plants are best suited to the different areas of your home:

- Low-light rooms
- Bathrooms and kitchens
- Bedrooms
- Office desks and spaces
- Large spaces
- Small spaces (including terrariums, hanging baskets and pots, wall planters and vertical gardens)

LOW-LIGHT ROOMS

Most plants prefer growing in a brightly lit room, out of direct sunlight; however, the following plants will tolerate dimly lit spaces and enable even dark corners of rooms to be filled with greenery:

* Cast iron plant (*Aspidistra elatior*)
* Chinese evergreen (*Aglaonema* spp.)
* Devil's ivy (*Epipremnum aureum*)
* Mother-in-law's tongue (*Sansevieria trifasciata*)
* Prayer plant (*Maranta leuconeura*)
* ZZ plant (*Zamioculcas zamiifolia*)

BATHROOMS AND KITCHENS

These plants prefer a humid location, so like growing in the moist or steamy environments that bathrooms and kitchens can provide:

- African mask plant (*Alocasia amazonica*)
- Arrowhead plant (*Syngonium podophyllum*)
- Devil's ivy (*Epipremnum aureum*)
- Flamingo flower (*Anthurium scherzerianum*)
- Hare's foot fern (*Davallia solida* var. *pyxidata*)
- Japanese aralia (*Fatsia japonica*)
- Kentia palm (*Howea forsteriana*)
- Maidenhair fern (*Adiantum aethiopicum*)
- Moth orchid (*Phalaenopsis* spp.)

- Parlour palm (*Chamaedorea elegans*)
- Peace lily (*Spathiphyllum wallisii*)
- Peacock plant (*Calathea* spp.)
- Prayer plant (*Maranta leuconeura*)
- Spider plant (*Chlorophytum comosum*)
- Waffle plant (*Hemigraphis alternata*)
- Zebra plant (*Aphelandra squarrosa*)
- ZZ plant (*Zamioculcas zamiifolia*)

LEFT: Peace lily
ABOVE: Moth orchid

BEDROOMS

We all want a soothing bedroom to escape to, and plants with soft-flowing or delicate foliage can help create a much more relaxed atmosphere. Consider growing some of the following plants for a little bit of bedroom calm:

- Arrowhead plant (*Syngonium podophyllum*)
- Chain of hearts (*Ceropegia woodii*)
- Devil's ivy (*Epipremnum aureum*)
- English ivy (*Hedera helix*)
- Heartleaf philodendron (*Philodendron scandens*)
- Hoya (*Hoya* spp.)
- Maidenhair fern (*Adiantum aethiopicum*)
- Mistletoe cactus (*Rhipsalis baccifera*)
- Spider plant (*Chlorophytum comosum*)
- String of pearls (*Senecio rowleyanus*)

ABOVE: Rubber plant

OFFICE DESKS AND SPACES

It's wonderful to be able to personalise our office desks, so along with photos of family and pets, why not add one of the following plants? They are all relatively compact and easy-care office desk choices that will tolerate air conditioning, indoor lighting and dry weekends, as well as making work hours more enjoyable:

- Baby rubber plant (*Peperomia obtusifolia*)
- Chinese evergreen (*Aglaonema* spp.)
- Corn plant (*Dracaena fragrans*)
- Jade plant (*Crassula ovata*)
- Moth orchid (*Phalaenopsis* spp.)
- Mother-in-law's tongue (*Sansevieria trifasciata*)
- Peace lily (*Spathiphyllum wallisii*)
- Rex begonia (*Begonia rex-cultorum*)
- Zebra cactus (*Haworthia fasciata*)
- ZZ plant (*Zamioculcas zamiifolia*)

And for larger office spaces, such as entrance foyers, common areas or on top of filing cabinets, these plants can add to office greenery:

- Arrowhead plant *(Syngonium podophyllum)*
- Cast iron plant *(Aspidistra elatior)*
- Devil's ivy *(Epipremnum aureum)*
- Heartleaf philodendron *(Philodendron scandens)*
- Philodendron *(Philodendron bipinnatifidum)*

LARGE SPACES

If you need to fill a corner of a room, create a tall leafy backdrop for other indoor plants or would love a bold tropical statement, then these large plants can provide an easy way to add instant jungle:

- African mask plant (*Alocasia amazonica*)
- Cast iron plant (*Aspidistra elatior*)
- China doll (*Radermachera sinica*)
- Corn plant (*Dracaena fragrans*)
- Dragon tree (*Dracaena marginata*)
- Fiddle leaf fig (*Ficus lyrata*)
- Japanese aralia (*Fatsia japonica*)
- Kentia palm (*Howea forsteriana*)
- Mother-in-law's tongue (*Sansevieria trifasciata*)
- Parlour palm (*Chamaedorea elegans*)
- Philodendron (*Philodendron bipinnatifidum*)
- Rubber plant (*Ficus elastica*)
- Swiss cheese plant (*Monstera deliciosa*)
- Umbrella tree (*Schefflera actinophylla*)
- Weeping fig (*Ficus benjamina*)
- ZZ plant (*Zamioculcas zamiifolia*)

LEFT: Rubber plant
RIGHT: Swiss cheese
    plant

SMALL SPACES

If space is at a premium, there's no need to forgo the dream of having a flourishing indoor garden. There are many pint-sized plants that are just perfect for small spaces; plants that can be grown in beautiful table top glass terrariums or ways of growing plants in vertical gardens that can utilise walls, and also hanging plants that really do make use of thin air!

SMALL PLANTS

These plants are naturally relatively small or can be kept compact with regular pruning:

- African violet (*Saintpaulia ionantha*)
- Air plants (*Tillandsia* spp.)
- Aloe vera (*Aloe barbadensis*)
- Baby rubber plant (*Peperomia obtusifolia*)
- Chinese money plant (*Pilea peperomioides*)
- Jade plant (*Crassula ovata*)
- Moth orchid (*Phalaenopsis* spp.)
- Nerve plant (*Fittonia* spp.)
- Polka dot plant (*Hypoestes phyllostachya*)
- Prayer plant (*Maranta leuconeura*)
- Zebra cactus (*Haworthia fasciata*)

TERRARIUMS

Terrariums, whether open or closed, are glass containers that are filled with small ecosystems of tiny plants. They can be low maintenance, are perfect for small spaces and can include the following plants:

- Air plants (*Tillandsia* spp.) (open terrariums)
- English ivy (*Hedera helix*)
- Hare's foot fern (*Davallia solida* var. *pyxidata*)
- Jade plant (*Crassula ovata*) (open terrariums)
- Maidenhair fern (*Adiantum aethiopicum*)
- Nerve plant (*Fittonia* spp.)

- Parlour palm (*Chamaedorea elegans*) (open terrariums)
- Polka dot plant (*Hypoestes phyllostachya*)
- Rex begonia (*Begonia rex-cultorum*)
- Spider plant (*Chlorophytum comosum*)

HANGING BASKETS AND POTS AND WALL PLANTERS

If you're short on space, hanging pots, baskets and wall planters provide a fantastic opportunity to make use of unused vertical spaces and add even more lushness to a room. They can also show off the cascading habit of arching or trailing plants. Create a great display with the following plants:

- Chain of hearts (*Ceropegia woodii*)
- Devil's ivy (*Epipremnum aureum*)
- Hare's foot fern (*Davallia solida* var. *pyxidata*)
- Heartleaf philodendron (*Philodendron scandens*)
- Hoya (*Hoya* spp.)
- Maidenhair fern (*Adiantum aethiopicum*)
- Mistletoe cactus (*Rhipsalis baccifera*)
- String of pearls (*Senecio rowleyanus*)

VERTICAL GARDENS

Bare walls are an ideal spot for installing a vertical garden. A lush green wall is soothing and helps to soften hard interior lines, plus a large number of plants can be grown in a small area. Different plants can be combined to create an interesting and fabulous green wall, and can include weeping, cascading and leafy foliage plants such as:

- Baby rubber plant (*Peperomia obtusifolia*)
- Devil's ivy (*Epipremnum aureum*)
- Flamingo flower (*Anthurium scherzerianum*)
- Hare's foot fern (*Davallia solida* var. *pyxidata*)
- Heartleaf philodendron (*Philodendron scandens*)
- Maidenhair fern (*Adiantum aethiopicum*)
- Mistletoe cactus (*Rhipsalis baccifera*)
- Peace lily (*Spathiphyllum wallisii*)
- Spider plant (*Chlorophytum comosum*)

PLANT ATTRIBUTES

Whether you're a beginner gardener, have very little time to look after plants, love succulents or the look of colourful flowers or foliage, there's an indoor plant to suit you. Here are some suggestions for plants that may match your skill level, amount of spare time and design dreams.

LOW-MAINTENANCE AND BEGINNER PLANTS

If you're just starting out with indoor gardening, believe you have a brown thumb or don't have a lot of time to devote to plant care, there are many plants that don't require too much maintenance and are more tolerant of neglect than other plants, including:

- Air plants (*Tillandsia* spp.)
- Aloe vera (*Aloe barbadensis*)
- Arrowhead plant (*Syngonium podophyllum*)
- Bromeliads
- Cast iron plant (*Aspidistra elatior*)
- Chinese evergreen (*Aglaonema* spp.)
- Corn plant (*Dracaena fragrans*)
- Devil's ivy (*Epipremnum aureum*)
- Dragon tree (*Dracaena marginata*)
- Heartleaf philodendron (*Philodendron scandens*)
- Hoya (*Hoya* spp.)
- Jade plant (*Crassula ovata*)
- Japanese aralia (*Fatsia japonica*)
- Mistletoe cactus (*Rhipsalis baccifera*)
- Mother-in-law's tongue (*Sansevieria trifasciata*)
- Peace lily (*Spathiphyllum wallisii*)
- Philodendron (*Philodendron bipinnatifidum*)
- Prayer plant (*Maranta leuconeura*)
- Rubber plant (*Ficus elastica*)
- Spider plant (*Chlorophytum comosum*)
- String of pearls (*Senecio rowleyanus*)
- Swiss cheese plant (*Monstera deliciosa*)
- Umbrella tree (*Schefflera actinophylla*)
- Zebra cactus (*Haworthia fasciata*)
- ZZ plant (*Zamioculcas zamiifolia*)

SUCCULENTS

Succulents are super popular, not only because of their impressive range of foliage colours and shapes, but also because they are usually low maintenance. Small succulents look fantastic when grown in eclectic or quirky pots. However, not all succulents are suitable for growing inside, as some require higher levels of light, so choose from the following list if you're keen on growing succulents indoors:

- Aloe vera *(Aloe barbadensis)*
- Jade plant *(Crassula ovata)*
- String of pearls *(Senecio rowleyanus)*
- Zebra cactus *(Haworthia fasciata)*

ABOVE: Jade plant

LEFT: Aloe vera & Chinese money plant

ABOVE: African violet

LEFT: Hoya

FLOWERS

Most of us think of indoor plants as being a sea of green; however, many also have beautiful and long-lasting flowers, adding another dimension to our indoor jungles. If you want to add flowering plants to your indoor garden, choose from the following:

- African violet (*Saintpaulia ionantha*)
- Bromeliads
- Flamingo flower (*Anthurium scherzerianum*)
- Hoya (*Hoya* spp.)
- Moth orchid (*Phalaenopsis* spp.)
- Peace lily (*Spathiphyllum wallisii*)
- Zebra plant (*Aphelandra squarrosa*)

ABOVE: Flamingo flower
RIGHT: Moth orchid

FOLIAGE

Interior spaces can be given extra pizzazz by including indoor plants with vibrant leaf colours and patterns. Foliage colours can be coordinated with décor and pots, or used to create a focal point on their own. Here are some indoor plant ideas 'beyond the green':

- African mask plant (*Alocasia amazonica*)
- Bromeliads
- Chain of hearts (*Ceropegia woodii*)
- Chinese evergreen (*Aglaonema* spp.)
- Croton (*Codiaeum variegatum*)
- Dumb cane (*Dieffenbachia* spp.)
- Nerve plant (*Fittonia* spp.)
- Never never plant (*Ctenanthe* spp.)
- Peacock plant (*Calathea* spp.)

- Polka dot plant (*Hypoestes phyllostachya*)
- Prayer plant (*Maranta leuconeura*)
- Rex begonia (*Begonia rex-cultorum*)
- Spider plant (*Chlorophytum comosum*)
- Waffle plant (*Hemigraphis alternata*)
- Watermelon peperomia (*Peperomia argyreia*)
- Zebra cactus (*Haworthia fasciata*)
- Zebra plant (*Aphelandra squarrosa*)

ABOVE: Croton

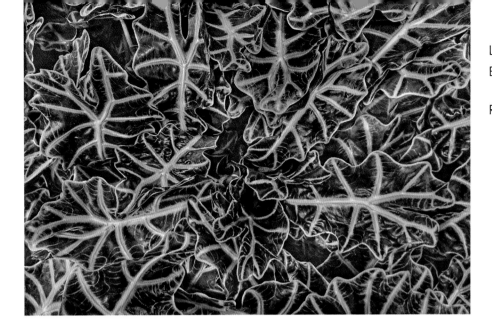

LEFT: African mask plant
BELOW: Watermelon peperomia
RIGHT: Nerve plant

IMPROVING INDOOR AIR QUALITY

In addition to benefiting mental and emotional wellbeing, all plants growing indoors have the ability to improve air quality, by filtering various pollutants and toxins. However, some plants have been studied more closely than others with respect to their ability to clean the air, with NASA and other researchers highlighting the following indoor plants as being particularly beneficial:

- Aloe vera (*Aloe barbadensis*)
- Bromeliads
- Chinese evergreen (*Aglaonema* spp.)
- Corn plant (*Dracaena fragrans*)
- Devil's ivy (*Epipremnum aureum*)
- Dumb cane (*Dieffenbachia* spp.)
- English ivy (*Hedera helix*)
- Ferns
- Flamingo flower (*Anthurium scherzerianum*)
- Hoya (*Hoya* spp.)
- Moth orchid (*Phalaenopsis* spp.)
- Mother-in-law's tongue (*Sansevieria trifasciata*)
- Palms
- Peace lily (*Spathiphyllum wallisii*)
- Philodendrons (*Philodendron*)
- Rubber plant (*Ficus elastica*)
- Spider plant (*Chlorophytum comosum*)
- Umbrella tree (*Schefflera actinophylla*)
- Waffle plant (*Hemigraphis alternata*)
- Weeping fig (*Ficus benjamina*)

The more plants you can include in your indoor spaces the better the air purifying effects will be. Choosing a range of plants is also beneficial, as they all have varying abilities to filter different toxins. It's also a scientifically valid reason to have lots of indoor plants!

During daylight hours, in a process called photosynthesis, plants will convert the sun's energy and carbon dioxide into nutrients they use for growth, and release oxygen into the atmosphere. At night time, most plants will absorb small amounts of oxygen and release carbon dioxide. Some plants use a slightly different mechanism, called CAM (Crassulacean Acid Metabolism) photosynthesis, where they will absorb carbon dioxide at night. Having plants in our bedrooms helps to create a more relaxed, sleep-conducive atmosphere, and indoor plants that use CAM photosynthesis can be grown in bedrooms, to help improve night time air quality. These unusual plants include:

- Aloe vera (*Aloe barbadensis*)
- Bromeliads
- Moth orchids (*Phalaenopsis* spp.)
- Mother-in-law's tongue (*Sansevieria trifasciata*)
- Air plants (*Tillandsia* spp.)
- Zebra cactus (*Haworthia fasciata*)
- ZZ plant (*Zamioculcas zamiifolia*)

ABOVE & LEFT: Swiss cheese plant

50 PLANTS

In this book, both the common name and the full scientific name (or genus) of the plant have been included, to help you avoid confusing one plant with another. For example, there are several plants with the word 'zebra' in their common name, and there are multiple philodendrons and ferns; some plants also have more than one common name. It's important to look at the care information for the particular plant you have, to give it the best possible chance of flourishing.

01

- Yates Premium Potting Mix
- Yates Thrive All Purpose Liquid Plant Food

AFRICAN MASK PLANT OR ELEPHANT'S EAR

Alocasia amazonica

The African mask plant doesn't come from Africa, nor from the Amazon, but from humid tropical forests in Asia and Australia. The deep green, serrated leathery leaves are shaped like an African mask, with distinctive thick white veins. They're fast growing plants that can reach up to 1m tall, creating a striking and exotic look when grown on their own or combined with plants with contrasting leaf shapes and colours.

HOW TO GROW:

1. Depending on the size of your plant, choose a pot around 5cm wider and taller than its current pot, with good drainage holes.
2. Position the pot in a warm, very brightly lit spot indoors that doesn't receive direct sunlight and is protected from cold draughts.
3. Half fill the pot with a quality potting mix, such as Yates Premium Potting Mix.
4. Remove the African mask plant from its container, position in the new pot and gently backfill with potting mix. The level of the potting mix should be the same as the original level of mix around the plant, so all the roots are covered.
5. Water well to settle the potting mix around the roots.
6. Keep the potting mix consistently slightly moist. Check moisture levels by inserting your finger into the top few centimetres of mix. If it feels dry, water the plant; if it's still moist, leave watering for a few days. Watering can be reduced during the cooler months.
7. To promote healthy foliage growth, from spring to autumn feed once a month with Yates Thrive All Purpose Liquid Plant Food.

GROWING TIPS:

- Gently dust the leaves regularly to keep them clean and healthy.
- They can stay in the same pot for several years.
- African mask plants love humidity and will enjoy having their foliage misted with water during hot dry weather; you can also sit the pot on a saucer of water that's filled with pebbles and regularly add water to the saucer.

02

RECOMMENDED PRODUCTS:

• Yates Thrive Roses & Flowers Liquid Plant Food

AFRICAN VIOLET

Saintpaulia ionantha

African violets are small plants with round, slightly hairy leaves and beautiful flowers that come in shades of blue, violet, burgundy, pink and white, with some having gorgeous double, ruffled or patterned petals. Some varieties also have striking cream or pink variegated leaves. African violets take up very little room and so are perfect plants for apartments and when you want to add pops of colour in among your leafy greens.

HOW TO GROW:

1. Choose a pot around 10cm wide that has good drainage holes. Specially designed ceramic self-watering or wicking pots are ideal for African violets.
2. Position the pot in a brightly lit spot that doesn't receive direct sunlight and is protected from draughts.
3. Half fill the pot with a quality, free draining African violet potting mix.
4. Remove the African violet from its container, position in the new pot and gently backfill with potting mix. The level of the potting mix should be the same as the original level of mix around the plant, so all the roots are covered but not any of the leaves or stems.
5. Water well to settle the potting mix around the roots.
6. African violets prefer to dry out slightly in between waterings. Check moisture levels by inserting your finger into the top few centimetres of mix. See below for the correct way to water an African violet.
7. To promote healthy leaf growth and lots of flowers, from spring to autumn feed every fortnight with half strength potassium enriched Yates Thrive Roses & Flowers Liquid Plant Food.

GROWING TIPS:

• Avoid wetting African violet foliage and stems. To water African violets, sit the pot in a saucer of lukewarm water for 15 minutes (or until all the potting mix is moist), then tip out the water from the saucer and allow the water to completely drain from the potting mix before returning the pot onto the saucer.
• Remove dead flowers and leaves regularly.
• Remove dust from the leaves by gently dusting with a small brush.
• African violets can be propagated from cuttings. Cut a leaf stem off at its base and insert the end into moist African violet potting mix.

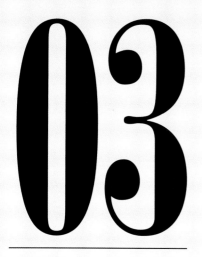

03

RECOMMENDED PRODUCTS:

- Yates Thrive Orchid Liquid Plant Food

AIR PLANTS

Tillandsia spp.

Air plants are a fascinating group of plants in the bromeliad family that are so named because of their ability to survive in air. Tillandsias are able to absorb moisture and nutrients from the atmosphere through their leaves and don't need to grow in soil. This means that air plants can be balanced, glued, wired, strung, placed or hung almost anywhere and take up very little room. Air plants originate from a diverse range of habitats, from deserts to tropical forests. They come in a wide variety of interesting leaf shapes, sizes, textures and colours, and some also have beautiful flowers. They're a perfect low maintenance plant for beginner gardeners if given the right amount of light and moisture.

HOW TO GROW:

1. Position the air plant in a brightly lit spot indoors that doesn't receive direct sunlight and is protected from draughts.
2. Air plants can be 'watered' each week from spring to autumn by soaking them in a bowl of water for 15 minutes. For air plants that can't be immersed in water (for example, if they are mounted on an object), they can be thoroughly misted with water. It's best to soak or mist in the mornings so the foliage has a chance to dry off before evening. During winter, reduce the soaking or misting to once a month.
3. To promote healthy growth, feed sparingly from spring to autumn once a month with Yates Thrive Orchid Liquid Plant Food, which can be mixed into the soaking or misting water.

GROWING TIPS:

- Air plants can be loosely placed in an open dry terrarium or bowl with decorative pebbles or sand, driftwood and shells.
- After flowering, some air plants will produce 'pups' (small new baby plants) that can be separated when they're about a third of the size of the original plant.
- Don't allow moisture to build up in the base of terrariums or bowls as air plants do not tolerate wet feet.

04

RECOMMENDED PRODUCTS:

• Yates Thrive All Purpose Liquid Plant Food

ALOE VERA
Aloe barbadensis

The aloe family of succulents contains hundreds of different species. One of the best known is aloe vera, which is used in skin and hair care products, health tonics and as a way to relieve minor burns. Aloe vera is a slow growing succulent with upright fleshy green leaves. Aloe vera don't mind dry air and, as they are able to store moisture in their leaves, they are tolerant of infrequent watering. They are a great low maintenance indoor plant for a bright location. Their upright growth means they don't take up much space, so they are perfect for a sunny shelf or windowsill.

HOW TO GROW:

1. Choose a pot at least 15cm wide that has good drainage holes.
2. Position the pot in a very brightly lit spot indoors that does not receive direct sunlight.
3. Half fill the pot with a quality, free draining cacti and succulent potting mix.
4. Remove the aloe vera plant from its container, position in the new pot and gently backfill with potting mix. The level of the potting mix should be the same as the original level of mix around the plant, so all the roots are covered.
5. Water well to settle the potting mix around the roots.
6. Aloe vera can dry out in between waterings. Check moisture levels by inserting your finger into the top few centimetres of mix. If it feels dry, water the plant; if it's still moist, leave watering for a few days. Watering can be reduced during the cooler months. Aloe vera does not like to be overwatered.
7. To promote healthy growth, from spring to autumn feed every month with Yates Thrive All Purpose Liquid Plant Food.

GROWING TIPS:

• To soothe minor burns, cut off a section of leaf and rub the sticky juice straight onto the burn.
• Aloe vera may produce 'pups' (small new baby plants) around the base, which can be carefully separated and planted into their own pot.

05

RECOMMENDED PRODUCTS:

• Yates Premium Potting Mix

• Yates Thrive All Purpose
  Liquid Plant Food

ARROWHEAD PLANT

Syngonium podophyllum

Also known as goosefoot plant, arrowhead plants are easy care plants with lush leaves on long creeping stems. They can be trained up a support to create a pillar of greenery, cascade out of a hanging basket or be grown in a pot and positioned where they can drape over a shelf. Many attractive variegated and coloured varieties are also available, including those with pale pink or silvery leaves, or yellow, white and cream spotted or marbled markings. Miniature arrowheads are perfect for terrariums.

HOW TO GROW:

1. Choose a pot or hanging basket at least 20cm wide that has good drainage holes.
2. Position the pot in a warm, brightly lit spot indoors that doesn't receive direct sunlight. Non-variegated and darker green coloured arrowhead plants will also tolerate more dimly lit positions.
3. Half fill the pot with a quality potting mix, such as Yates Premium Potting Mix.
4. Remove the arrowhead plant from its container, position in the new pot and gently backfill with potting mix. The level of the potting mix should be the same as the original level of mix around the plant, so all the roots are covered.
5. Water well to settle the potting mix around the roots.
6. Allow the top few centimetres of potting mix to dry out slightly before rewatering. Check moisture levels by inserting your finger into the top few centimetres of mix. If it feels dry, water the plant; if it's still moist, leave watering for a few days.
7. To promote healthy foliage growth, from spring to autumn feed once a fortnight with Yates Thrive All Purpose Liquid Plant Food.

GROWING TIPS:

*   Gently dust the leaves regularly to keep them clean and healthy.
*   To keep arrowhead plants more compact and bushy, trim stems to the desired length. Use the cut pieces to propagate more plants: insert a 15cm length of stem that contains a node (a bump on the stem) into moist potting mix and roots will develop in a few weeks.
*   Arrowhead plants can stay in the same pot for several years.
*   They like humidity so do well in bathrooms or can have their foliage regularly misted with water.

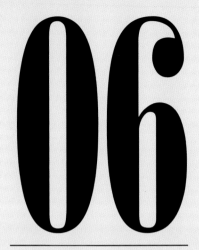

BABY RUBBER PLANT

Peperomia obtusifolia

Baby rubber plants, sometimes called pepper face, are compact, low maintenance plants with rounded, glossy, thick succulent-like leaves. They create a lovely foliage contrast when grouped with strappy, erect or feathery leaved plants, and some baby rubber plant varieties have attractive yellow variegated leaves or red tinged stems. Only reaching around 30cm tall, they are perfectly suited to growing where space is limited and make wonderful office desk plants or great shelf fillers when planted in a shallow bowl; they also look good in a hanging basket.

RECOMMENDED PRODUCTS:

- Yates Premium Potting Mix
- Yates Thrive All Purpose Liquid Plant Food

HOW TO GROW:

1. Choose a pot at least 15cm wide, or slightly larger than the existing pot, that has good drainage holes.
2. Position the pot in a well-lit spot indoors that doesn't receive direct sunlight. Baby rubber plants will also tolerate more dimly lit positions.
3. Half fill the pot with a quality potting mix, such as Yates Premium Potting Mix.
4. Remove the baby rubber plant from its container, position in the new pot and gently backfill with potting mix. The level of the potting mix should be the same as the original level of mix around the plant, so all the roots are covered but not any of the leaves.
5. Water well to settle the potting mix around the roots.
6. The top few centimetres of potting mix can be allowed to dry out in between waterings. Check moisture levels by inserting your finger into the top few centimetres of mix. If it feels dry, water the plant; if it's still moist, leave watering for a few days. Baby rubber plants don't like to be waterlogged.
7. To promote healthy foliage growth, from spring to autumn feed every month with Yates Thrive All Purpose Liquid Plant Food.

GROWING TIPS:

- For more compact, bushier plants, regularly pinch out the stem tips.
- Variegated varieties will require a brighter spot to do well.
- Remove any dead leaves to keep the plant looking tidy.
- Avoid watering the leaves, which can cause marks. Water the soil around the plant.

07

RECOMMENDED PRODUCTS:

- Yates Thrive Orchid Liquid Plant Food

BROMELIADS

Bromeliads (which also include pineapples and Spanish moss) are native to tropical areas in the Americas where they're often found growing up in the tree canopy. They come in a range of interesting leaf arrangements, shapes, sizes, colours and patterns, including stripes, splotches and spots, in shades of lime green, grey, burgundy, pink and yellow. Many will also produce vibrant, long lasting flowers (which are actually modified leaves called bracts). They make fantastic, low maintenance indoor plants for brightly lit spaces, adding a bold tropical feel to a bedroom or office desk.

HOW TO GROW:

1. A bromeliad will be happy in the same pot for several years; however, when they need a new or improved home, choose a pot at least 15cm wide that has good drainage holes.
2. Position the pot in a brightly lit spot indoors that doesn't receive direct sunlight.
3. Half fill the pot with a quality, free draining potting mix. A chunky orchid potting mix is ideal for bromeliads.
4. Remove the bromeliad from its container, position in the new pot and gently backfill with potting mix. The level of the potting mix should be the same as the original level of mix around the plant, so all the roots are covered.
5. Water well to settle the potting mix around the roots.
6. Keep the potting mix slightly moist. Check moisture levels by inserting your finger into the top few centimetres of mix. If it feels dry, water the plant by filling the central 'cup' with water until it overflows. This cup can be kept constantly filled with water during the warmer months.
7. To promote healthy growth, from spring to autumn feed every month with half strength Yates Thrive Orchid Liquid Plant Food.

GROWING TIPS:

- Bromeliads love humidity so their foliage can be misted regularly with water during hot dry weather.
- Many bromeliads will produce 'pups' (small new baby plants) that can be separated when they're about a third of the size of the original plant and planted into their own pot, where they'll start to grow their own roots.

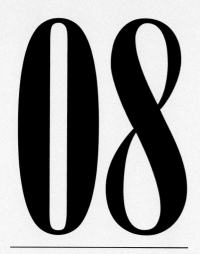

CAST IRON PLANT
Aspidistra elatior

As the name suggests, this is one tough character. Cast iron plants will tolerate low levels of light, moisture and humidity, and handle draughts, cool conditions and dust, and still appear lush and tropical, so it's a perfect indoor plant for beginner gardeners or serial plant neglecters! Cast iron plants have long, spear-shaped, dark green or yellow variegated leaves that can grow up to 90cm long. They tend to grow upright rather than spread, so they're great plants for filling a dark corner of a room or adding height to an indoor plant collection; they will also handle a breezy entrance or hallway.

RECOMMENDED PRODUCTS:

- Yates Premium Potting Mix
- Yates Thrive All Purpose Liquid Plant Food

HOW TO GROW:

1. Choose a pot at least 20cm wide that has good drainage holes.
2. Cast iron plants will do best in a brightly lit spot indoors that doesn't receive direct sunlight; however, they will also tolerate more dimly lit positions.
3. Half fill the pot with a quality potting mix, such as Yates Premium Potting Mix.
4. Remove the cast iron plant from its container, position in the new pot and gently backfill with potting mix. The level of the potting mix should be the same as the original level of mix around the plant, so all the roots are covered.
5. Water well to settle the potting mix around the roots.
6. Keep the potting mix only slightly moist. Check moisture levels by inserting your finger into the top few centimetres of mix. If it feels dry, water the plant; if it's still moist, leave watering for a few days. Cast iron plants do not like to be overwatered and will tolerate becoming dry in between waterings.
7. To promote lush healthy foliage growth, from spring to autumn feed every month with Yates Thrive All Purpose Liquid Plant Food.

GROWING TIPS:

- Cut any dead leaves off at the base of the stem to keep the plant looking tidy.
- Cast iron plants are fairly slow growing and can stay in the same pot for several years. Once the plant has outgrown its current pot, divide and separate and plant into new pots during spring or summer.
- Despite being super tough, cast iron plants will appreciate their foliage being misted with water during hot dry weather.

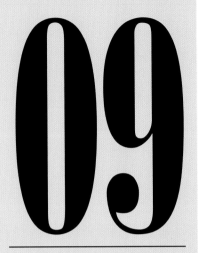

RECOMMENDED PRODUCTS:

- Yates Premium Potting Mix
- Yates Thrive Houseplant Liquid Plant Food
- Yates Seed Raising Mix

CHAIN OF HEARTS

Ceropegia woodii

Chain of hearts, also known as rosary vine, is a gorgeous trailing plant that's perfect for cascading out of small hanging pots or baskets. The 'chains' can reach several metres long and the delicate looking, succulent-like green and red heart-shaped leaves are so sweet. Chain of hearts can even flower indoors, producing unusual small pink tubular blooms. They look fantastic when grouped together with other trailing plants such as string of pearls or mistletoe cactus or provide a great contrast to upright leafy plants displayed on shelves.

HOW TO GROW:

1. Choose a pot at least 10cm wide that has good drainage holes.
2. Position the pot in a very brightly lit spot that's protected from draughts. Chain of hearts will tolerate some direct morning sunlight but not harsh midday or afternoon sun.
3. Half fill the pot with a quality, free draining potting mix such as Yates Premium Potting Mix.
4. Remove the chain of hearts from its container, position in the new pot and gently backfill with potting mix. The level of the potting mix should be the same as the original level of mix around the plant, so all the roots are covered.
5. Water well to settle the potting mix around the roots.
6. Chain of hearts prefers to dry out in between waterings. Check moisture levels by inserting your finger into the top few centimetres of mix. If it feels dry, water the plant; if it's still moist, leave watering for a few days. Watering can be reduced during the cooler months.
7. To promote healthy growth, from spring to autumn feed every month with Yates Thrive Houseplant Liquid Plant Food.

GROWING TIPS:

- Chain of hearts doesn't develop dense leaves and stems, but to help keep it a little more compact, the long stems can be trimmed to the desired length.
- Chain of hearts can be propagated by laying a length of stem on top of Yates Seed Raising Mix. Keep moist, and roots can grow from stem nodes (where leaves emerge from the stem).

10

CHINA DOLL

Radermachera sinica

When grown indoors, China doll has masses of small glossy green leaves and looks like a lush miniature tree. Growing up to 1.5m tall, they're wonderful plants for screening or dividing room spaces or can be grouped with contrasting smaller plants to create an eye-catching designer look.

HOW TO GROW:

1. Choose a pot at least 20cm wide that has good drainage holes.
2. Position the pot in a very brightly lit spot indoors that doesn't receive direct sunlight and is protected from draughts.
3. Half fill the pot with a quality potting mix, such as Yates Premium Potting Mix.
4. Remove the China doll from its container, position in the new pot and gently backfill with potting mix. The level of the potting mix should be the same as the original level of mix around the plant, so all the roots are covered.
5. Water well to settle the potting mix around the roots.
6. Keep the potting mix slightly moist, particularly during the warmer months. Check moisture levels by inserting your finger into the top few centimetres of mix. If it feels dry, water the plant; if it's still moist, leave watering for a few days. China doll does not like to be overwatered.
7. To promote healthy foliage growth, from spring to autumn feed every 2 weeks with Yates Thrive All Purpose Liquid Plant Food.

GROWING TIPS:

• China doll plants can shed their leaves if they're moved, so it's best to leave the plant in the one spot.
• It can live in the same pot for several years as it doesn't mind becoming a bit pot bound.
• To keep China doll compact and bushy, pinch out the tips of the tallest stems.
• These plants like humidity and will enjoy having their foliage misted with water, particularly during hot dry weather.

11

CHINESE EVERGREEN

Aglaonema spp.

Chinese evergreens are a wonderfully diverse and colourful range of slow growing, clump forming leafy plants that are native to tropical and subtropical areas in Asia. Their foliage can be striking mottled mixtures of red, pink, silver, green, yellow or cream and the plant can be used to bring life and colour to your indoor spaces. A variety of different coloured species of Chinese evergreens can be grouped together to create an attractive foliage display; they also look fantastic when grown alongside other indoor plants with contrasting foliage shapes.

RECOMMENDED PRODUCTS:

- Yates Premium Potting Mix
- Yates Thrive All Purpose Liquid Plant Food

HOW TO GROW:

1. Choose a pot at least 25cm wide, or only slightly larger than the existing pot, that has good drainage holes.
2. Position the pot in a warm, brightly lit spot indoors that doesn't receive direct sunlight, and that is protected from cold draughts. Chinese evergreens will also tolerate more dimly lit positions.
3. Half fill the pot with a quality potting mix, such as Yates Premium Potting Mix.
4. Remove the Chinese evergreen from its container, position in the new pot and gently backfill with potting mix. The level of the potting mix should be the same as the original level of mix around the plant, so all the roots are covered.
5. Water well to settle the potting mix around the roots.
6. The top few centimetres of the potting mix can be allowed to dry out slightly in between waterings. Check moisture levels by inserting your finger into the top few centimetres of mix. If it feels dry, water the plant; if it's still moist, leave watering for a few days. Watering can be reduced during the cooler months. Chinese evergreens do not like to be waterlogged.
7. To promote healthy and colourful foliage growth, from spring to autumn feed monthly with Yates Thrive All Purpose Liquid Plant Food.

GROWING TIPS:

- These plants are slow growing and can stay in the same pot for several years.
- The lighter the foliage colour, the brighter the location will need to be (but still out of direct sunlight).
- It does not like the cold and needs warm conditions to flourish.

12

- Yates Premium Potting Mix
- Yates Thrive All Purpose Liquid Plant Food

CHINESE MONEY PLANT

Pilea peperomioides

Chinese money plants, also known as pancake plants or simply pilea, have become a hot item for collectors and indoor plant enthusiasts. Native to China, they have round green leaves up to 10cm in diameter growing from an upright central stem. Reaching up to 30cm tall, pilea's interesting leaves make it a wonderful feature plant on its own or when combined with different plants with contrasting foliage.

HOW TO GROW:

1. Choose a pot at least 20cm wide that has good drainage holes. Pileas look great in simple terracotta pots.
2. Position the pot in a brightly lit spot indoors that doesn't receive direct sunlight.
3. Half fill the pot with a quality, free draining potting mix, such as Yates Premium Potting Mix.
4. Remove the pilea from its container, position in the new pot and gently backfill with potting mix. The level of the potting mix should be the same as the original level of mix around the plant, so all the roots are covered.
5. Water well to settle the potting mix around the roots.
6. Keep the potting mix slightly moist, particularly during the warmer months. Check moisture levels by inserting your finger into the top few centimetres of mix. If it feels dry, water the plant; if it's still moist, leave watering for a few days. Pilea doesn't like wet feet so it's important not to overwater.
7. To promote healthy foliage growth, from spring to autumn feed every 2 weeks with Yates Thrive All Purpose Liquid Plant Food.

GROWING TIPS:

- Trim off any dead leaves to keep the plant looking tidy and gently dust or wipe the leaves to remove any dust.
- Baby pileas may sprout up around the mother plant and can be gently cut off a few centimetres below the soil surface and potted into their own pots.
- Rotate your pilea pot by 90–180 degrees each week, to promote even access to sunlight and encourage more symmetrical growth.

13

RECOMMENDED PRODUCTS:

- Yates Premium Potting Mix
- Yates Thrive All Purpose Liquid Plant Food

CORN PLANT
Dracaena fragrans

Corn plants, or sometimes delightfully called 'happy plants', develop thick upright woody stems that can grow several metres tall and are topped with long arching foliage. The broad leaves can be green or have yellow stripes. Corn plants can grow into a large and leafy focal point, particularly when grown in clumps with stems cut to different lengths, which creates a lush tiered foliage effect. Perfect to fill the corner of a room, corn plants require little maintenance and help to improve indoor air quality.

HOW TO GROW:

1. Depending on the size of your plant, choose a pot around 5cm wider and taller than its current pot, with good drainage holes.
2. Position the pot in a brightly lit spot indoors that doesn't receive direct sunlight. Corn plants will also tolerate more dimly lit positions.
3. Half fill the pot with a quality potting mix, such as Yates Premium Potting Mix.
4. Remove the corn plant from its container, position in the new pot and gently backfill with potting mix. The level of the potting mix should be the same as the original level of mix around the plant, so all the roots are covered.
5. Water well to settle the potting mix around the roots.
6. The top few centimetres of the potting mix can be allowed to dry out slightly in between waterings. Check moisture levels by inserting your finger into the top few centimetres of mix. If it feels dry, water the plant; if it's still moist, leave watering for a few days. Watering can be reduced during the cooler months. Corn plants do not like to be waterlogged.
7. To promote healthy foliage growth, from spring to autumn feed once a month with Yates Thrive All Purpose Liquid Plant Food.

GROWING TIPS:

- Happy corn plants can sometimes flower, producing sprays of white, beautifully fragrant flowers.
- If your corn plant becomes too tall, you can cut the woody stem at the desired height and new leaves will develop below the cut. You can also insert the cut piece into moist potting mix, to grow a brand new plant.
- Varieties with coloured foliage need a brighter location to retain their colouring (but still out of direct sunlight).
- Corn plants are slow growing and can stay in the same pot for several years.

14

CROTON
Codiaeum variegatum

Crotons, sometimes called Joseph's coat, have intensely colourful waxy foliage. Colours include vibrant reds and pinks, bright yellow, rich orange, cream, white and deep green in almost every pattern and combination, with some plants having multiple colours on the one plant. Different varieties can have pencil thin or large elliptical leaves and some have wavy leaf edges or the leaves are completely curled. Crotons can be a little temperamental if they're not grown in their ideal environment; however, their kaleidoscope of exotic tropical colours makes them well worth trying.

RECOMMENDED PRODUCTS:

- Yates Premium Potting Mix
- Yates Thrive All Purpose Liquid Plant Food

HOW TO GROW:

1. Depending on the size of your plant, choose a pot around 5cm wider and taller than its current pot, with good drainage holes.
2. Position the pot in a warm, very brightly lit spot indoors that doesn't receive direct sunlight and is protected from cold draughts.
3. Half fill the pot with a quality potting mix, such as Yates Premium Potting Mix.
4. Remove the croton from its container, taking care not to disturb the roots. Position in the new pot and gently backfill with potting mix. The level of the potting mix should be the same as the original level of mix around the plant, so all the roots are covered but not any of the leaves.
5. Water well to settle the potting mix around the roots.
6. Keep the potting mix consistently moist. Check moisture levels by inserting your finger into the top few centimetres of mix. If it feels dry, water the plant; if it's still moist, leave watering for a few days.
7. To promote healthy colourful foliage growth, from spring to autumn feed every fortnight with Yates Thrive All Purpose Liquid Plant Food.

GROWING TIPS:

- Crotons need a brightly lit spot to maintain their colourful foliage.
- For more compact, bushier plants, regularly pinch out the stem tips.
- Croton plants don't like being moved and can lose some (or all) of their leaves when you take a new plant home or relocate an existing plant. New leaves will emerge once you find their ideal spot.
- Crotons like warmth and humidity and will enjoy having their foliage misted with water during hot dry weather.

15

- Yates Premium Potting Mix
- Yates Thrive All Purpose Liquid Plant Food

DEVIL'S IVY OR GOLDEN POTHOS

Epipremnum aureum

Devil's ivy can be your go-to plant when you're starting on your indoor plant journey. It's tough, will tolerate low levels of light, requires little maintenance and still looks fantastic. It's a versatile, trailing or climbing plant with heart-shaped leaves that can cascade out of a hanging basket or it can be grown in a pot and trained up supports or along walls and shelves using picture hooks or string. The pot itself needn't take up much room yet the plant can still create metres of wonderful greenery.

HOW TO GROW:

1. Choose a pot or hanging basket at least 20cm wide, or only slightly larger than the existing pot, that has good drainage holes.
2. Position the pot in a brightly lit spot indoors that doesn't receive direct sunlight; however, devil's ivy will also tolerate more dimly lit positions.
3. Half fill the pot with a quality potting mix, such as Yates Premium Potting Mix.
4. Remove the devil's ivy from its container, position in the new pot and gently backfill with potting mix. The level of the potting mix should be the same as the original level of mix around the plant, so all the roots are covered.
5. Water well to settle the potting mix around the roots.
6. The potting mix can be allowed to dry out slightly in between waterings. Check moisture levels by inserting your finger into the top few centimetres of mix. If it feels dry, water the plant; if it's still moist, leave watering for a few days. Watering can be reduced during the cooler months. Devil's ivy does not like to be waterlogged.
7. To promote healthy foliage growth, from spring to autumn feed once a month with Yates Thrive All Purpose Liquid Plant Food.

GROWING TIPS:

- For a more compact, bushier plant, the tips of stems can be trimmed. Place these cuttings into moist potting mix or a glass of water to create new plants.
- Devil's ivy can stay in the same pot for several years.
- Variegated devil's ivy varieties are available, with attractive mottled yellow or cream colours. To retain their colours, these varieties need a brighter location than pure green devil's ivy.

16

RECOMMENDED PRODUCTS:

- Yates Premium Potting Mix
- Yates Thrive Houseplant Liquid Plant Food

DRAGON TREE

Dracaena marginata

If you're after a dramatic plant that brings an eye-catching desert or minimalist look indoors, then a dragon tree is for you. They have thin pointed leaves which predominantly stand bold and erect in massed clumps on top of slender woody stems that can reach 2–3m tall. Varieties are available in various foliage colours, including yellow, cream, green, purple and red stripes, so they make a bold statement indoors.

HOW TO GROW:

1. Depending on the size of your plant, choose a pot around 5cm wider and taller than its current pot, with good drainage holes.
2. Position the pot in a brightly lit spot indoors that doesn't receive direct sunlight.
3. Half fill the pot with a quality potting mix, such as Yates Premium Potting Mix.
4. Remove the dragon tree from its container, position in the new pot and gently backfill with potting mix. The level of the potting mix should be the same as the original level of mix around the plant, so all the roots are covered.
5. Water well to settle the potting mix around the roots.
6. The top few centimetres of the potting mix can be allowed to dry out slightly in between waterings. Check moisture levels by inserting your finger into the top few centimetres of mix. If it feels dry, water the plant; if it's still moist, leave watering for a few days. Watering can be reduced during the cooler months. Dragon trees do not like to be waterlogged.
7. To promote healthy and colourful foliage growth, from spring to autumn feed once a month with Yates Thrive Houseplant Liquid Plant Food.

GROWING TIPS:

- Gently dust the leaves regularly to keep them clean and healthy.
- If your dragon tree becomes too tall, you can cut the woody stem at the desired height and new leaves will develop below the cut. You can also insert the cut piece into moist potting mix, to grow a brand new plant.
- Dragon trees don't mind being pot bound and can stay in the same pot for several years.

17

DUMB CANE
Dieffenbachia spp.

Despite having the unfortunate name of dumb cane (due to its potential to cause speaking and breathing difficulties if ingested), dieffenbachias have very attractive large yellow and green patterned leaves and bring a lovely lush, tropical feel indoors. Different varieties have varying and beautiful foliage patterns, ranging from green with pale mottling to pale yellow rimmed with a green edge, with most dieffenbachias growing to around 60cm tall.

HOW TO GROW:

1. Choose a pot at least 20cm wide that has good drainage holes.
2. Position the pot in a warm, brightly lit spot indoors that doesn't receive direct sunlight and is protected from draughts.
3. Half fill the pot with a quality potting mix, such as Yates Premium Potting Mix.
4. Remove the dieffenbachia from its container, position in the new pot and gently backfill with potting mix. The level of the potting mix should be the same as the original level of mix around the plant, so all the roots are covered.
5. Water well to settle the potting mix around the roots.
6. Keep the potting mix consistently moist, particularly during the warmer months. Check moisture levels by inserting your finger into the top few centimetres of mix. If it feels dry, water the plant; if it's still moist, leave watering for a few days.
7. To promote healthy and colourful foliage growth, from spring to autumn feed every month with Yates Thrive All Purpose Liquid Plant Food.

GROWING TIPS:

• Remove any dead leaves to keep the plant looking tidy.
• Dust or gently wipe the leaves regularly to remove any dust.
• Dieffenbachia can be propagated by taking stem cuttings during the warmer months.

18

ENGLISH IVY
Hedera helix

English ivy is often overlooked as an option for growing indoors, with many people shying away from it due to its reputation for being invasive and smothering buildings and trees. However, contained in a pot, it's a wonderful indoor plant with elegant trailing stems and distinctive multi-pointed leaves. It's ideal for growing in a hanging basket, where it can cascade lushly over the edges, or it can be trained up a decorative support.

RECOMMENDED PRODUCTS:

- Yates Premium Potting Mix
- Yates Thrive All Purpose Liquid Plant Food

HOW TO GROW:

1. Choose a pot or hanging basket at least 15cm wide that has good drainage holes.
2. Position the pot in a brightly lit spot indoors that doesn't receive direct sunlight.
3. Half fill the pot with a quality potting mix, such as Yates Premium Potting Mix.
4. Remove the ivy from its container, position in the new pot and gently backfill with potting mix. The level of the potting mix should be the same as the original level of mix around the plant, so all the roots are covered.
5. Water well to settle the potting mix around the roots.
6. Ivy can dry out slightly in between waterings. Check moisture levels by inserting your finger into the top few centimetres of mix. If it feels dry, water the plant; if it's still moist, leave watering for a few days. Watering can be reduced during the cooler months.
7. To promote healthy growth, from spring to autumn feed every month with Yates Thrive All Purpose Liquid Plant Food.

GROWING TIPS:

- Do not allow ivy to touch walls or other household surfaces as it can attach roots and cause damage.
- During hot and dry weather, ivy leaves can be misted with water.
- To help keep the ivy more bushy and compact, the long stems can be trimmed to the desired length.
- Ivy can be easily propagated by taking a 10cm stem cutting and inserting into moist potting mix.

19

RECOMMENDED PRODUCTS:

- Yates Premium Potting Mix
- Yates Thrive All Purpose Liquid Plant Food

FIDDLE LEAF FIG

Ficus lyrata

If you want to create a bold statement, then fiddle leaf figs are the indoor plant for you. These tall plants with super-sized leaves add instant tropical lushness to a room, and look fantastic all on their own or as a glossy green backdrop for smaller plants.

HOW TO GROW:

1. Depending on the size of your plant, choose a pot around 5cm wider and taller than its current pot, with good drainage holes.
2. Position the pot in a brightly lit spot indoors that doesn't receive direct sunlight and is protected from cold draughts.
3. Half fill the pot with a quality potting mix, such as Yates Premium Potting Mix.
4. Carefully remove the fiddle leaf fig from its container. Position in the new pot and gently backfill with potting mix. The level of the potting mix should be the same as the original level of mix around the plant, so all the roots are covered.
5. Water well to settle the potting mix around the roots.
6. Keep the potting mix consistently slightly moist. Check moisture levels by inserting your finger into the top few centimetres of mix. If it feels dry, water the plant; if it's still moist, leave watering for a few days. Fiddle leaf figs like to be moist but not overwatered.
7. To promote lush healthy foliage growth, from spring to autumn feed every 2 weeks with Yates Thrive All Purpose Liquid Plant Food.

GROWING TIPS:

- The large foliage can attract dust, which should be gently wiped or dusted off.
- Promote bushier growth by pinching out the top of the stem.
- During hot dry weather, fiddle leaf figs will appreciate their foliage being misted with water.
- Fiddle leaf figs can be left in the same pot for several years, until roots start to emerge from the base of the pot.
- Although not as temperamental as other figs, avoid moving fiddle leaf figs, as a change in environment can cause the leaves to drop.
- Rotate your fig pot by 90–180 degrees every few weeks, to promote even access to sunlight and encourage more symmetrical growth.

20

RECOMMENDED PRODUCTS:

- Yates Premium Potting Mix
- Yates Thrive Roses & Flowers Liquid Plant Food

FLAMINGO FLOWER

Anthurium scherzerianum

Anthuriums feature brightly coloured 'flowers' (technically known as spathes) in a range of vibrant colours including rich red, pretty pinks, light green, deep purple and white, with a long distinctive 'spadix' (a spike of minute flowers) growing from the base of the flower. The waxy looking heart-shaped flowers are long lasting and can be cut for a vase. Anthuriums also have lush green foliage that grows to around 60cm tall; however, it's the tropical looking flowers that steal the show.

HOW TO GROW:

1. Choose a pot at least 20cm wide that has good drainage holes.
2. Position the pot in a warm, brightly lit spot indoors that doesn't receive direct sunlight and is protected from draughts.
3. Half fill the pot with a quality potting mix, such as Yates Premium Potting Mix.
4. Remove the anthurium from its container, position in the new pot and gently backfill with potting mix. The level of the potting mix should be the same as the original level of mix around the plant, so all the roots are covered.
5. Water well to settle the potting mix around the roots.
6. Allow the potting mix to dry out slightly between waterings. Anthuriums do not like to be overwatered. Check moisture levels by inserting your finger into the top few centimetres of mix. If it feels dry, water the plant; if it's still moist, leave watering for a few days.
7. To promote healthy foliage growth and lots of gorgeous flowers, from spring to autumn feed every 2 weeks with potassium enriched Yates Thrive Roses & Flowers Liquid Plant Food.

GROWING TIPS:

- Anthuriums like humidity so their foliage can be misted regularly with water, particularly during hot dry weather.
- Remove any dead leaves and flowers to keep the plant looking tidy and to promote more flowers.
- The foliage can attract dust, which should be gently wiped or dusted off.

21

- Yates Premium Potting Mix

- Yates Thrive All Purpose
  Liquid Plant Food

HARE'S FOOT FERN

Davallia solida var. pyxidata

Native to rainforest areas, this interesting fern has long, furry creeping stems (rhizomes) that grow on top of the soil and look like a hare's foot. These hairy stems can become quite an eye-catching feature as they creep over the edge of a pot or hanging basket. Hare's foot fern has lush foliage which looks wonderful when grown alongside other ferns with different leaf shapes or mixed with other leafy indoor plants.

HOW TO GROW:

1. Choose a pot at least 20cm wide that has good drainage holes.
2. Position the pot in a brightly lit spot indoors that doesn't receive direct sunlight and is protected from draughts.
3. Half fill the pot with a quality potting mix, such as Yates Premium Potting Mix.
4. Remove the fern from its container, position in the new pot and gently backfill with potting mix. The level of the potting mix should be the same as the original level of mix around the plant, so all the roots are covered but not any of the leaves or furry rhizomes.
5. Water well to settle the potting mix around the roots.
6. It's very important to keep the potting mix consistently moist, but not soggy. Check moisture levels by inserting your finger into the top few centimetres of mix. If it feels dry, quickly water the plant! If it's still moist, leave watering for a few days.
7. To promote healthy foliage growth, from spring to autumn feed once a month with Yates Thrive All Purpose Liquid Plant Food.

GROWING TIPS:

- To keep the fern looking tidy, cut back any damaged or dead fronds at the base.
- Hare's foot ferns like humidity so their foliage and furry rhizomes can be misted regularly with water, particularly during hot dry weather.
- To create a more humid environment around the fern, you can sit the pot on a saucer of water that's filled with pebbles and regularly add water to the saucer.

22

HEARTLEAF PHILODENDRON

Philodendron scandens

This climbing philodendron is an ideal plant for beginner indoor gardeners, as it's tough, forgiving, and still looks fantastically lush. It has heart-shaped glossy green leaves that grow on stems several metres long and can either be grown as a climber up a support or can cascade out of a pot or hanging basket. It's a fantastic trailing plant for a shelf, where it can spill down and around books and ornaments. Attractive variegated types have yellow or cream stripes or splotches on their leaves.

RECOMMENDED PRODUCTS:

- Yates Premium Potting Mix
- Yates Thrive All Purpose Liquid Plant Food

HOW TO GROW:

1. Choose a pot or hanging basket at least 20cm wide that has good drainage holes.
2. Position the pot in a brightly lit spot indoors that doesn't receive direct sunlight. Heartleaf philodendron will also tolerate more dimly lit positions.
3. Half fill the pot with a quality potting mix, such as Yates Premium Potting Mix.
4. Remove the philodendron from its container, position in the new pot and gently backfill with potting mix. The level of the potting mix should be the same as the original level of mix around the plant, so all the roots are covered.
5. Water well to settle the potting mix around the roots.
6. Allow the top few centimetres of potting mix to dry out before rewatering. Check moisture levels by inserting your finger into the top few centimetres of mix. If it feels dry, water the plant; if it's still moist, leave watering for a few days.
7. To promote healthy foliage growth, from spring to autumn feed once a month with Yates Thrive All Purpose Liquid Plant Food.

GROWING TIPS:

- Gently dust the leaves regularly to keep them clean and healthy.
- To keep this philodendron more compact, the stems can be trimmed to the desired length. You can use the cut pieces to propagate more plants. Simply insert a 15cm length of stem that contains a node (a bump on the stem) into moist potting mix and roots will develop.
- Heartleaf philodendrons can stay in the same pot for several years.

23

- Yates Premium Potting Mix
- Yates Thrive Roses & Flowers Liquid Plant Food

HOYA

Hoya spp.

Sometimes called wax plants or wax flowers, hoyas are vines native to tropical areas in Asia and Australia. They have thick succulent-like leaves on long stems, with some varieties having variegated, curled or slightly hairy leaves. Hardy and low maintenance, hoyas have clusters of flowers (see page 44) in shades of pink, burgundy, purple, cream, yellow or white; many are fragrant. They look brilliant spilling from hanging baskets.

HOW TO GROW:

1. Hoyas can be left in the same pot for several years; however, if they need a new home, choose a pot or hanging basket around 20cm wide that has good drainage holes.
2. Position the pot in a brightly lit spot that doesn't receive direct sunlight and is protected from draughts. Bright, indirect light is the key to getting hoyas to flower.
3. Half fill the pot with a quality, free draining potting mix, such as Yates Premium Potting Mix.
4. Remove the hoya from its container, being careful not to disturb the roots, position in the new pot and gently backfill with potting mix. The level of the potting mix should be the same as the original level of mix around the plant, so all the roots are covered.
5. Water well to settle the potting mix around the roots.
6. The potting mix can be allowed to dry out slightly in between waterings. Check moisture levels by inserting your finger into the top few centimetres of mix. If it feels dry, water the plant; if it's still moist, leave watering for a few days. Hoyas do not like to be waterlogged.
7. To promote healthy foliage and lots of flowers, from spring to autumn feed fortnightly with Yates Thrive Roses & Flowers Liquid Plant Food.

GROWING TIPS:

- Create more plants by laying stems, still attached to the plant, over moist potting mix, where they will form roots in a few months. You may need to pin the stems down to ensure good contact with the potting mix. Rooted stems can be cut off and planted into their own pots.
- Don't cut off old flower stems as new flowers will grow from the same spot, and don't move a flowering hoya as the flowers can fall off.

24

* Yates Thrive Houseplant Liquid Plant Food

JADE PLANT

Crassula ovata

Also known as the money plant, this hardy African succulent is reported to bring good luck. Maturing into the shape of a small tree with a brown woody trunk, jade plants have thick, glossy leaves and are a great low maintenance plant for office desks and warm windowsills, and also make brilliant bonsai plants.

HOW TO GROW:

1. Choose a pot at least 15cm wide that has good drainage holes.
2. Position the pot in a very brightly lit spot indoors that ideally does receive some direct sunlight.
3. Half fill the pot with a quality, free draining cacti and succulent potting mix.
4. Remove the jade plant from its container, position in the new pot and gently backfill with potting mix. The level of the potting mix should be the same as the original level of mix around the plant, so all the roots are covered.
5. Water well to settle the potting mix around the roots.
6. Keep the potting mix only slightly moist. Check moisture levels by inserting your finger into the top few centimetres of mix. If it feels dry, water the plant; if it's still moist, leave watering for a few days. Watering can be reduced during the cooler months. Jade plants do not like to be overwatered.
7. To promote healthy growth, from spring to autumn feed every month with half strength Yates Thrive Houseplant Liquid Plant Food.

GROWING TIPS:

* Jade plants will live quite happily for many years in the same pot, though they can become quite top heavy with age.
* To help promote denser growth, ensure the jade plant is growing in a well-lit position, and regularly prune stem tips.
* It can be easily propagated by taking individual leaves, letting them dry out for a few days and then gently pushing the stem end into slightly moist cacti and succulent mix. Roots will form within a few months.

25

JAPANESE ARALIA

Fatsia japonica

Also called the paper plant, Japanese aralia has large glossy leaves with finger-like lobes and can grow to 2m tall. It can be used as a tall backdrop in a collection of different plants with varying leaf shapes and colours or as a bold statement plant on its own. Japanese aralia is hardy and will tolerate quite cool conditions indoors, so it's a fantastic plant for people living in colder areas or for rooms that are not heated during winter.

HOW TO GROW:

1. Depending on the size of your plant, choose a pot around 5cm wider and taller than its current pot, with good drainage holes. The larger the pot, the larger the plant will grow, so consider this when choosing a pot.
2. Position the pot in a brightly lit spot indoors that doesn't receive direct sunlight and is protected from draughts.
3. Half fill the pot with a quality potting mix, such as Yates Premium Potting Mix.
4. Remove the Japanese aralia from its container, position in the new pot and gently backfill with potting mix. The level of the potting mix should be the same as the original level of mix around the plant, so all the roots are covered.
5. Water well to settle the potting mix around the roots.
6. Japanese aralias like to be kept consistently moist during the warmer months. Check moisture levels by inserting your finger into the top few centimetres of mix. If it feels dry, water the plant; if it's still moist, leave watering for a few days.
7. To promote healthy foliage growth, from spring to autumn feed every fortnight with Yates Thrive All Purpose Liquid Plant Food.

GROWING TIPS:

- Gently dust the large leaves regularly to keep them clean and healthy.
- To keep Japanese aralia bushy and more compact, the growing tips can be trimmed. Or if the plant becomes too big for its spot, the whole plant can be cut back by a third. Use the cuttings to create more plants.
- Japanese aralias will enjoy having their foliage misted with water during hot dry weather.

26

KENTIA PALM

Howea forsteriana

Native to Australia's Lord Howe Island, kentia palms are slow growing palms with graceful, arching dark green fronds. Indoors they will grow up to around 2m tall and are very attractive tropical looking plants that can create a statement on their own or can be grouped with other potted plants with contrasting foliage colours and shapes. As they are large plants, they can be used effectively to create instant indoor greenery, screen areas within rooms or fill a bare corner. Kentia palms like humidity and make fantastic lush bathroom plants.

RECOMMENDED PRODUCTS:

- Yates Premium Potting Mix
- Yates Thrive All Purpose Liquid Plant Food

HOW TO GROW:

1. Choose a pot at least 30cm wide that has good drainage holes.
2. Position the pot in a moderately to brightly lit spot indoors that doesn't receive direct sunlight.
3. Half fill the pot with a quality potting mix, such as Yates Premium Potting Mix.
4. Carefully remove the kentia palm from its container and don't disturb the roots. Position in the new pot and gently backfill with potting mix. The level of the potting mix should be the same as the original level of mix around the plant, so all the roots are covered.
5. Water well to settle the potting mix around the roots.
6. Keep the potting mix only slightly moist. Check moisture levels by inserting your finger into the top few centimetres of mix. If it feels dry, water the plant; if it's still moist, leave watering for a few days. Kentia palms do not like to be overwatered.
7. To promote lush healthy foliage growth, from spring to autumn feed every month with Yates Thrive All Purpose Liquid Plant Food.

GROWING TIPS:

- Kentia palms like humidity so their foliage can be misted regularly with water during hot dry weather. This will also help to remove dust, which can accumulate on the leaves.
- They can be left in the same pot for several years, as they are slow growers and dislike root disturbance.
- Remove any dead fronds to keep the plant looking tidy.

27

MAIDENHAIR FERN

Adiantum aethiopicum

Soft, feathery light green foliage is one of the charms of maidenhair ferns. They have a reputation for being difficult to grow; however, providing the correct levels of light and moisture is key to keeping these ferns happy and flourishing. Their graceful leafy stems arch up and out from the base of the plant, cascading gently over the edges of the pot, so they're ideal for hanging baskets. They love a humid bathroom or the shelter of a moist terrarium and can also provide a lovely delicate contrast to hard surfaces and plants with rigid foliage.

RECOMMENDED PRODUCTS:

- Yates Premium Potting Mix
- Yates Thrive All Purpose Liquid Plant Food

HOW TO GROW:

1. Choose a pot at least 20cm wide that has good drainage holes. Self-watering pots are a great choice for maidenhair ferns as they can draw from the water reservoir as they need it.
2. Position the pot in a brightly lit spot indoors that doesn't receive direct sunlight and is protected from draughts.
3. Half fill the pot with a quality potting mix, such as Yates Premium Potting Mix.
4. Remove the fern from its container, position in the new pot and gently backfill with potting mix. The level of the potting mix should be the same as the original level of mix around the plant, so all the roots are covered but not any of the stems or leaves.
5. Water well to settle the potting mix around the roots.
6. It's very important to keep the potting mix consistently moist, but not soggy. Check moisture levels by inserting your finger into the top few centimetres of mix. If it feels dry, quickly water the plant! If it's still moist, leave watering for a few days.
7. To promote healthy foliage growth, from spring to autumn feed once a month with Yates Thrive All Purpose Liquid Plant Food.

GROWING TIPS:

- To keep the fern looking tidy, cut back any damaged or dead fronds at the base.
- Maidenhair ferns like humidity so their foliage can be misted regularly with water, particularly during hot dry weather.
- To create a more humid environment around the fern, you can sit the pot on a saucer of water that's filled with pebbles and regularly add water to the saucer.

28

RECOMMENDED PRODUCTS:

• Yates Thrive Houseplant
Liquid Plant Food

MISTLETOE CACTUS
Rhipsalis baccifera

With its long, thin and weeping fleshy green stems, mistletoe cactus does not look or behave like a traditional cactus at all. Coming from tropical rainforests, it prefers a protected, humid environment and doesn't like direct sunlight. Its trailing habit makes it a perfect plant for vertical gardens and hanging baskets or it can be grown on a shelf and allowed to cascade over the edge. Mistletoe cactus's interesting slender, weeping stems create a great contrast when grown alongside indoor plants with round or coloured foliage.

HOW TO GROW:

1. Choose a pot or hanging basket at least 15cm wide that has good drainage holes.
2. Position the pot in a brightly lit spot indoors that doesn't receive direct sunlight.
3. Half fill the pot with a quality, free draining cacti and succulent potting mix.
4. Remove the mistletoe cactus from its container, position in the new pot and gently backfill with potting mix. The level of the potting mix should be the same as the original level of mix around the plant, so all the roots are covered.
5. Water well to settle the potting mix around the roots.
6. Keep the potting mix only slightly moist. Check moisture levels by inserting your finger into the top few centimetres of mix. If it feels dry, water the plant; if it's still moist, leave watering for a few days. Watering can be reduced during the cooler months.
7. To promote healthy growth, from spring to autumn feed every month with Yates Thrive Houseplant Liquid Plant Food.

GROWING TIPS:

• Mistletoe cactus can be propagated by taking 10cm stem cuttings during the warmer months and inserting the ends into cacti and succulent mix. Roots will form within 1–2 months.
• During hot dry weather, mistletoe cactus stems can be misted regularly with water.

29

RECOMMENDED PRODUCTS:

- Yates Thrive Orchid Liquid Plant Food

MOTH ORCHID
Phalaenopsis spp.

Moth orchids are native to tropical forests in Asia, where they usually live up in the tree canopy, attaching themselves to trunks and growing in branch forks. They're popular flowering gifts as they have long arching stalks laden with multiple flowers that can last for months. They come in a wide range of beautiful colours including almost every shade of pink, mauve, salmon, yellow, white and burgundy as well as striking multi-coloured or spotted flowers. Coming from the tropics, they love humidity and grow beautifully in a brightly lit bathroom. They also make a stunning table centrepiece when in glorious full bloom.

HOW TO GROW:

1. A moth orchid will be happy in the same well drained pot for several years. However, if they need a new or improved home, choose a pot around 15cm wide that has good drainage holes.
2. Position the pot in a warm, brightly lit spot indoors that doesn't receive direct sunlight and is protected from draughts.
3. Half fill the pot with a quality chunky orchid potting mix.
4. Remove the orchid from its container, position in the new pot and gently backfill with orchid mix. The level of the orchid mix should be the same as the original level of mix around the plant, so all the roots are covered but not any of the leaves.
5. Water well to settle the potting mix around the roots.
6. Allow the orchid mix to slightly dry out in between waterings. Check moisture levels by inserting your finger into the top few centimetres of mix. If it feels dry, apply some water to the mix, avoiding wetting the leaves of the orchid.
7. To promote healthy leaf growth and flowers, feed every 2–4 weeks with Yates Thrive Orchid Liquid Plant Food.

GROWING TIPS:

- Moth orchid roots don't like to be constantly wet, so don't let the plant sit in a saucer of water.
- After flowering, prune back the flower stem to just above the second node (bump on the stem) from the base. Keep the flower support stake and clips to use for the next flower stalk.

30

MOTHER-IN-LAW'S TONGUE

Sansevieria trifasciata

Mother-in-law's tongue (also called snake plant or viper's bowstring hemp) is a type of succulent with long, upright, sword-shaped variegated leaves. Their strong bold look creates a striking focal point and their erect growth makes them a great plant for narrow spaces. These are super tough plants and, despite being a succulent, will tolerate quite low levels of light indoors. They're slow growing, require minimal maintenance and will handle becoming dry in between waterings. Sansevierias are also fantastic for improving indoor air quality.

RECOMMENDED PRODUCTS:

- Yates Premium Potting Mix
- Yates Thrive Houseplant Liquid Plant Food

HOW TO GROW:

1. Choose a pot at least 20cm wide that has good drainage holes.
2. Position the pot in a brightly lit spot indoors that doesn't receive direct sunlight; however, mother-in-law's tongue will also tolerate a dimly lit position.
3. Half fill the pot with a quality potting mix, such as Yates Premium Potting Mix.
4. Remove the mother-in-law's tongue from its container, position in the new pot and gently backfill with potting mix. The level of the potting mix should be the same as the original level of mix around the plant, so all the roots are covered.
5. Water well to settle the potting mix around the roots.
6. Allow the potting mix to dry out almost completely before re-watering. Check moisture levels by inserting your finger into the top few centimetres of mix.
7. To promote healthy foliage growth, from spring to autumn feed every month with Yates Thrive Houseplant Liquid Plant Food.

GROWING TIPS:

- Mother-in-law's tongue does not like wet feet, so ensure it's growing in a well-drained pot and is not overwatered.
- Re-pot every couple of years to help keep it flourishing.
- You can propagate mother-in-law's tongue by taking leaf cuttings during the warmer months or dividing the clumps.

31

NERVE PLANT
Fittonia spp.

Nerve plants have very attractive dark green leaves with distinctive white, cream or dark pink veins and patterns. They're compact plants with a spreading habit, only growing to around 15cm tall, and growing several varieties of nerve plants together creates a vibrant, colourful display. They come from tropical forests in South America and their small size and love of humidity also makes them perfect terrarium plants.

RECOMMENDED PRODUCTS:

- Yates Premium Potting Mix
- Yates Thrive All Purpose Liquid Plant Food

HOW TO GROW:

1. Choose a pot at least 10cm wide, or only slightly larger than the existing pot, that has good drainage holes.
2. Position the pot in a warm, well-lit spot indoors that doesn't receive direct sunlight and is protected from draughts.
3. Part fill the pot with a quality potting mix, such as Yates Premium Potting Mix.
4. Remove the nerve plant from its container, position in the new pot and gently backfill with potting mix. The level of the potting mix should be the same as the original level of mix around the plant, so all the roots are covered but not any of the leaves.
5. Water well to settle the potting mix around the roots.
6. Keep the potting mix consistently slightly moist. Check moisture levels by inserting your finger into the top few centimetres of mix. If it feels dry, water the plant. If it's still moist, leave watering for a few days. Nerve plants do not like to be waterlogged.
7. To promote healthy colourful foliage growth, from spring to autumn feed once a fortnight with Yates Thrive All Purpose Liquid Plant Food.

GROWING TIPS:

- Nerve plants can be a bit fussy and like constant moisture and humidity, however are well worth growing for their beautifully coloured leaves.
- They will enjoy having their foliage misted with water during hot dry weather and you can also sit the pot on a saucer of water that's filled with pebbles and regularly add water to the saucer.
- Low light levels can reduce leaf colouring.
- For more compact, bushier plants, regularly pinch out the stem tips.
- Nerve plants can be propagated by taking a 10cm piece of stem and inserting it into moist potting mix. Roots should form in a few weeks.

32

RECOMMENDED PRODUCTS:

- Yates Premium Potting Mix
- Yates Thrive All Purpose Liquid Plant Food

NEVER NEVER PLANT

Ctenanthe spp.

There are several *Ctenanthe* species that make beautiful indoor plants, with striking patterned or coloured leaves on plants that can grow between 20 and 90cm tall. Their long, oval-shaped leaves can be silvery, green or burgundy and can have prominent and different coloured veins, splashes of pink or cream, distinct dark markings or rich purple colouring on the underside. As they love humidity, ctenanthes are ideal plants for adding colour to a brightly lit bathroom or to create foliage contrast in among green leafy indoor plants.

HOW TO GROW:

1. Choose a pot at least 20cm wide that has good drainage holes.
2. Position the pot in a warm, brightly lit spot indoors that doesn't receive direct sunlight and is protected from cold draughts.
3. Half fill the pot with a quality potting mix, such as Yates Premium Potting Mix.
4. Remove the plant from its container, position in the new pot and gently backfill with potting mix. The level of the potting mix should be the same as the original level of mix around the plant, so all the roots are covered but not any of the leaves.
5. Water well to settle the potting mix around the roots.
6. Keep the potting mix moist, particularly during the warmer months. Check moisture levels by inserting your finger into the top few centimetres of mix. If it feels dry, water the plant; if it's still moist, leave watering for a few days.
7. To promote healthy colourful foliage growth, from spring to autumn feed every 2 weeks with Yates Thrive All Purpose Liquid Plant Food.

GROWING TIPS:

- Ctenanthes love humidity so their foliage can be regularly misted with water, particularly during hot dry weather, or place their pot on a saucer of water that's filled with pebbles and regularly add water to the saucer.
- Remove any dead leaves to keep the plant looking tidy.
- Ctenanthes don't mind becoming slightly pot bound, so they can stay in the same pot for a few years.

33

PARLOUR PALM
Chamaedorea elegans

The name 'parlour palm' has a distinctly old-fashioned ring to it but these are perfect palms for modern day small spaces such as office desks, bathrooms and windowsills. Their arching fronds have small, delicate, green leaflets and they're usually grown in clumps, enhancing their lush, tropical appearance. They can grow up to around 1.5m tall; however, they are slow growers and can take many years to reach this height. Very young parlour palms can even be grown in open terrariums, adding a dense leafy vertical backdrop when combined with low growing terrarium plants.

RECOMMENDED PRODUCTS:

- Yates Premium Potting Mix
- Yates Thrive All Purpose Liquid Plant Food

HOW TO GROW:

1. Choose a pot at least 20cm wide that has good drainage holes.
2. Position the pot in a moderately to brightly lit spot indoors that doesn't receive direct sunlight.
3. Half fill the pot with a quality potting mix, such as Yates Premium Potting Mix.
4. Carefully remove the parlour palm from its container and don't disturb the roots. Position in the new pot and gently backfill with potting mix. The level of the potting mix should be the same as the original level of mix around the plant, so all the roots are covered.
5. Water well to settle the potting mix around the roots.
6. Keep the potting mix only slightly moist. Check moisture levels by inserting your finger into the top few centimetres of mix. If it feels dry, water the plant; if it's still moist, leave watering for a few days. Parlour palms do not like to be overwatered.
7. To promote lush healthy foliage growth, from spring to autumn feed every month with Yates Thrive All Purpose Liquid Plant Food.

GROWING TIPS:

- Parlour palms like humidity so their foliage can be misted regularly with water during hot dry weather. This will also help to remove dust, which can accumulate on the leaves.
- They can be left in the same pot for several years as they are slow growers and dislike root disturbance.
- Remove any dead fronds to keep the plant looking tidy.

34

RECOMMENDED PRODUCTS:

- Yates Premium Potting Mix
- Yates Thrive Roses & Flowers Liquid Plant Food

PEACE LILY

Spathiphyllum wallisii

The peace lily remains one of the most beautiful and popular indoor plants for good reason. They have dark green, tropical looking foliage, are hardy, produce tall white flowers and will even tell you when it's time to water by drooping their foliage. A perfect plant for beginner indoor gardeners! They also help clean the air and are fantastic plants for adding a lush feel to a humid bathroom or moderately lit bedroom.

HOW TO GROW:

1. Choose a pot at least 20cm wide that has good drainage holes.
2. Position the pot in a brightly lit spot indoors that doesn't receive direct sunlight; however, peace lilies will also tolerate more dimly lit positions. Protect from draughts.
3. Half fill the pot with a quality potting mix, such as Yates Premium Potting Mix.
4. Remove the peace lily from its container, position in the new pot and gently backfill with potting mix. The level of the potting mix should be the same as the original level of mix around the plant, so all the roots are covered but not any of the leaves.
5. Water well to settle the potting mix around the roots.
6. Keep the potting mix moist, particularly during the warmer months. Check moisture levels by inserting your finger into the top few centimetres of mix. If it feels dry, water the plant; if it's still moist, leave watering for a few days. Peace lily foliage will wilt if the plant needs watering; however, drooping foliage can also be a sign of waterlogged potting mix so check moisture levels with your finger first.
7. To promote healthy foliage growth and lots of flowers, from spring to autumn feed every 2 weeks with potassium enriched Yates Thrive Roses & Flowers Liquid Plant Food.

GROWING TIPS:

- Create new peace lilies by dividing crowded clumps and re-potting the smaller sections into their own pots.
- Peace lilies like humidity so their foliage can be misted regularly with water during hot dry weather.
- Remove any dead leaves and flowers to keep the plant looking tidy.

35

PEACOCK PLANT OR ZEBRA PLANT

Calathea spp.

Calatheas, often called peacock, zebra or rattlesnake plants, are a diverse group of tropical rainforest plants with wonderfully decorative foliage. Some species have distinct bold dark markings or beautiful white patterns and many have rich burgundy colouring on the underside of their leaves. Leaf shapes also range from narrow and elongated to large and oval, with plants growing up to 60cm tall. Calatheas are fantastic plants for adding colour to a bright bathroom, and upright varieties are perfect for limited spaces like shelves, benches and desks.

RECOMMENDED PRODUCTS:

- Yates Premium Potting Mix
- Yates Thrive All Purpose Liquid Plant Food

HOW TO GROW:

1. Choose a pot at least 20cm wide that has good drainage holes.
2. Position the pot in a brightly lit spot indoors that doesn't receive direct sunlight and is protected from cold draughts.
3. Half fill the pot with a quality potting mix, such as Yates Premium Potting Mix.
4. Remove the calathea from its container, position in the new pot and gently backfill with potting mix. The level of the potting mix should be the same as the original level of mix around the plant, so all the roots are covered but not any of the leaves.
5. Water well to settle the potting mix around the roots.
6. Keep the potting mix moist, particularly during the warmer months. Check moisture levels by inserting your finger into the top few centimetres of mix. If it feels dry, water the plant; if it's still moist, leave watering for a few days.
7. To promote healthy colourful foliage growth, from spring to autumn feed every 2 weeks with Yates Thrive All Purpose Liquid Plant Food.

GROWING TIPS:

- Calatheas love humidity so their foliage can be misted regularly with water, particularly during hot dry weather.
- Remove any dead leaves to keep the plant looking tidy.

36

PHILODENDRON

Philodendron bipinnatifidum

The retro look of philodendron, also called the tree philodendron or *Philodendron selloum*, is gloriously back in vogue. Popular in the 1970s, it's experiencing a revival due to it being a fast growing, easy care indoor plant with instant jungle appeal. It has interesting large glossy green leaves with long finger-like projections. The plant can grow up to 2m tall on a thick, woody stem, bringing an impressive tropical feel to indoor spaces.

HOW TO GROW:

1. Depending on the size of your plant, choose a pot around 5cm wider and taller than its current pot, with good drainage holes. The larger the pot, the larger the plant will grow, so consider this when choosing a pot.
2. Position the pot in a brightly lit spot indoors that doesn't receive direct sunlight and is protected from draughts.
3. Half fill the pot with a quality potting mix, such as Yates Premium Potting Mix. If growing up a post or support, it's a good idea to place the support in the pot when you're filling it with potting mix.
4. Remove the philodendron from its container, position in the new pot and gently backfill with potting mix. The level of the potting mix should be the same as the original level of mix around the plant, so all the roots are covered.
5. Water well to settle the potting mix around the roots.
6. Tree philodendrons like to be kept consistently moist. Check moisture levels by inserting your finger into the top few centimetres of mix. If it feels dry, water the plant; if it's still moist, leave watering for a few days.
7. To promote healthy foliage growth, from spring to autumn feed once a month with Yates Thrive All Purpose Liquid Plant Food.

GROWING TIPS:

- Gently dust the leaves regularly to keep them clean and healthy.
- These plants can grow quickly. If the plant becomes too large, the stems can be trimmed to keep the plant at the desired size. Use cut leaves as a long lasting, lush looking vase display.
- Philodendrons will enjoy having their foliage misted with water during hot dry weather.

37

POLKA DOT PLANT
Hypoestes phyllostachya

Polka dot or freckle face plants are small but spectacularly colourful plants with patterned soft foliage in shades of burgundy, pink, green, cream, red and white. Their intense colours team beautifully with leafy green ferns and they make ideal terrarium plants. They can also create an eye-catching display when grown in brightly coloured pots to match their vibrant foliage colours.

RECOMMENDED PRODUCTS:

- Yates Premium Potting Mix
- Yates Thrive All Purpose Liquid Plant Food

HOW TO GROW:

1. Choose a pot at least 15cm wide that has good drainage holes.
2. Position the pot in a warm, brightly lit spot indoors that doesn't receive direct sunlight.
3. Half fill the pot with a quality potting mix, such as Yates Premium Potting Mix.
4. Remove the polka dot plant from its container, position in the new pot and gently backfill with potting mix. The level of the potting mix should be the same as the original level of mix around the plant, so all the roots are covered but not any of the leaves.
5. Water well to settle the potting mix around the roots.
6. Keep the potting mix consistently slightly moist. Check moisture levels by inserting your finger into the top few centimetres of mix. If it feels dry, water the plant; if it's still moist, leave watering for a few days. Polka dot plants do not like to be waterlogged.
7. To promote healthy colourful foliage growth, from spring to autumn feed once a month with Yates Thrive All Purpose Liquid Plant Food.

GROWING TIPS:

- Polka dot plants are not as long lived as other indoor plants; however, they are well worth growing for their gorgeous colours.
- For more compact, bushier plants, regularly pinch out the stem tips. Low light conditions will lead to lanky growth.
- Polka dot plants can be propagated by taking a 10cm piece of stem and inserting it into moist potting mix. Roots should form in a few weeks.
- Polka dot plants like humidity and will enjoy having their foliage misted with water during hot dry weather; you can also sit the pot on a saucer of water that's filled with pebbles and regularly add water to the saucer.

38

RECOMMENDED PRODUCTS:

- Yates Premium Potting Mix
- Yates Thrive All Purpose Liquid Plant Food

PRAYER PLANT

Maranta leuconeura

Prayer plants are low growing leafy plants with fabulously coloured and patterned oval-shaped foliage. Some varieties have distinct red or white veined leaves; others have eye-catching dark spots and markings. Prayer plants are closely related to peacock plants (*Calathea* spp.) and both can often be incorrectly labelled. Growing to around 30cm tall, they don't take up much room so are perfect for creating colour and interest in smaller indoor spaces. A very interesting ability that prayer plants have is to raise their leaves up at night, as if in prayer (hence their name). So don't be alarmed that your prayer plant foliage moves by itself!

HOW TO GROW:

1. Choose a pot at least 20cm wide, or slightly larger than the existing pot, that has good drainage holes.
2. Position the pot in a warm, brightly lit spot indoors that doesn't receive direct sunlight and is protected from cold draughts. Prayer plants will also tolerate more dimly lit positions.
3. Half fill the pot with a quality potting mix, such as Yates Premium Potting Mix.
4. Remove the prayer plant from its container, position in the new pot and gently backfill with potting mix. The level of the potting mix should be the same as the original level of mix around the plant, so all the roots are covered but not any of the leaves.
5. Water well to settle the potting mix around the roots.
6. Keep the potting mix consistently moist, particularly during the warmer months. Check moisture levels by inserting your finger into the top few centimetres of mix. If it feels dry, water the plant; if it's still moist, leave watering for a few days.
7. To promote healthy colourful foliage growth, from spring to autumn feed every 2 weeks with Yates Thrive All Purpose Liquid Plant Food.

GROWING TIPS:

- Prayer plants like humidity so their foliage can be misted regularly with water during hot dry weather. Alternatively, place a layer of pebbles in a saucer, add water and position the prayer plant pot on the pebbles, so the base of the pot is sitting above the water. Keep the water around the pebbles topped up; this helps create a more humid environment for the plant.

39

RECOMMENDED PRODUCTS:

- Yates Premium Potting Mix
- Yates Thrive All Purpose Liquid Plant Food

REX BEGONIA

Begonia rex-cultorum

Rex begonias have amazingly coloured foliage in shades of red, orange, burgundy, pink, silver, grey and green. Combine this with incredible leaf patterns, shapes, spots, splotches, variegations, textures and whorls, and rex begonias are stunning houseplants. They look incredible when grouped together with different rex begonias but also work wonderfully when grown among green leafy plants. They don't grow much taller than 30cm, so are ideal for bringing vibrant colour to small spaces like shelves, table tops and office desks.

HOW TO GROW:

1. Choose a pot at least 15cm wide, or slightly larger than the existing pot, that has good drainage holes.
2. Position the pot in a warm, brightly lit spot indoors that doesn't receive direct sunlight and is protected from cold draughts. They will also grow well in fluorescent lighting.
3. Half fill the pot with a quality potting mix, such as Yates Premium Potting Mix.
4. Remove the begonia from its container, position in the new pot and gently backfill with potting mix. The level of the potting mix should be the same as the original level of mix around the plant, so all the roots are covered but not any of the leaves.
5. Water well to settle the potting mix around the roots.
6. Allow the top few centimetres of potting mix to dry out slightly before re-watering. Check moisture levels by inserting your finger into the top few centimetres of mix. If it feels dry, water the plant; if it's still moist, leave watering for a few days. Avoid wetting begonia foliage as this can promote diseases.
7. To promote healthy colourful foliage growth, from spring to autumn feed every month with Yates Thrive All Purpose Liquid Plant Food.

GROWING TIPS:

- Rex begonias can be left in the same pot for a few years as they don't mind being slightly pot bound.
- Remove any dead leaves to keep the plant looking tidy; long leggy stems can also be trimmed back.

40

RECOMMENDED PRODUCTS:

- Yates Premium Potting Mix
- Yates Thrive All Purpose Liquid Plant Food

RUBBER PLANT

Ficus elastica

Rubber plants have been grown as indoor plants for decades. Part of their popularity may be due to the fact that they require minimal maintenance and are fairly hard to kill. Rubber plants are tall and fast growing indoor plants with large glossy leaves. Some varieties have striking dark burgundy new foliage and stems; others have cream or pink variegated leaves. Their size makes them great plants to use for instant indoor greening, adding height in a mix of other plants or for screening off areas within a room.

HOW TO GROW:

1. Depending on the size of your plant, choose a pot around 5cm wider and taller than its current pot, with good drainage holes.
2. Position the pot in a brightly lit spot indoors that doesn't receive direct sunlight and is protected from draughts.
3. Half fill the pot with a quality potting mix, such as Yates Premium Potting Mix.
4. Carefully remove the rubber plant from its container. Position in the new pot and gently backfill with potting mix. The level of the potting mix should be the same as the original level of mix around the plant, so all the roots are covered.
5. Water well to settle the potting mix around the roots.
6. Keep the potting mix consistently slightly moist. Check moisture levels by inserting your finger into the top few centimetres of mix. If it feels dry, water the plant; if it's still moist, leave watering for a few days. Watering can be reduced during the cooler months.
7. To promote lush healthy foliage growth, from spring to autumn feed every 2 weeks with Yates Thrive All Purpose Liquid Plant Food.

GROWING TIPS:

- The large leaves can attract dust, which should be gently wiped or dusted off.
- Rubber plants can grow quickly, so may need to be re-potted every few years into a larger pot or back into the same pot after removing some of the roots and adding fresh potting mix.
- To keep the plant at a manageable height or to promote bushier growth, the tips of the stems can be pruned (avoid contact with the white sap).

41

- Yates Premium Potting Mix

- Yates Thrive Houseplant Liquid Plant Food

SPIDER PLANT

Chlorophytum comosum

Spider plants seemed to lose favour after their 1970s boom; however, they're making a serious and well deserved comeback. They're hardy, fast growing plants with attractive ribbons of variegated foliage. Their arching habit makes them perfect for growing in a hanging basket or a pot placed on a stand or shelf, where you can get the full cascading foliage effect. Spider plants help to improve air quality and are great for humid bathrooms, as well as being low maintenance office desk plants.

HOW TO GROW:

1. Choose a pot or hanging basket at least 20cm wide that has good drainage holes.
2. Position the pot in a brightly lit spot indoors that doesn't receive direct sunlight and is protected from draughts.
3. Half fill the pot with a quality potting mix, such as Yates Premium Potting Mix.
4. Remove the spider plant from its container, position in the new pot and gently backfill with potting mix. The level of the potting mix should be the same as the original level of mix around the plant, so all the roots are covered but not any of the leaves.
5. Water well to settle the potting mix around the roots.
6. Spider plants will tolerate drying out slightly in between waterings; however, they do best in moist potting mix. Check moisture levels by inserting your finger into the top few centimetres of mix. If it feels dry, water the plant; if it's still moist, leave watering for a few days. Spider plants do not like to be waterlogged.
7. To promote healthy foliage growth, from spring to autumn feed once a month with Yates Thrive Houseplant Liquid Plant Food.

GROWING TIPS:

- Cut back any damaged or dead leaves at the base.
- Spider plants can stay in the same pot for several years.
- Spider plants can produce long stems that grow mini spider plants on them. While still attached to the stem, place the mini spider plants on the top of moist soil, where they will form roots. They can then be cut off the stem and potted into their own container. Congested clumps can also be divided.

STRING OF PEARLS

Senecio rowleyanus

Whether you think they look like small peas or green pearls threaded onto strings, string of pearls is such an unusual looking plant that it's worth growing just for the wow factor. It's a type of succulent with long trailing stems that can reach up to a metre in length. They're perfect for hanging baskets, where they can cascade over the edges, forming a fascinating beaded green curtain, or they can spill out and over shelves and plant stands. String of pearls also looks stunning when combined with other indoor succulents with different leaf shapes.

HOW TO GROW:

1. Choose a pot at least 15cm wide that has good drainage holes.
2. Position the pot in a brightly lit spot indoors that doesn't receive direct sunlight.
3. Half fill the pot with a quality, free draining cacti and succulent potting mix.
4. Remove the string of pearls from its container, position in the new pot and gently backfill with potting mix. The level of the potting mix should be the same as the original level of mix around the plant, so all the roots are covered but not any of the stems or pearls.
5. Water well to settle the potting mix around the roots.
6. String of pearls prefers to dry out in between waterings. Check moisture levels by inserting your finger into the top few centimetres of mix. If it feels dry, water the plant; if it's still moist, leave watering for a few days. Watering can be reduced during the cooler months. String of pearls does not like to be overwatered.
7. To promote healthy growth, from spring to autumn feed every month with Yates Thrive Houseplant Liquid Plant Food.

GROWING TIPS:

• To help promote a denser, multi-stemmed plant, tip prune regularly.
• It can be easily propagated by taking 5cm stem cuttings during spring and summer and inserting the ends into slightly moist cacti and succulent mix. Roots will form within a few months.

43

SWISS CHEESE PLANT

Monstera deliciosa

Also called the fruit salad plant, *Monstera deliciosa* is the plant to grow when you want to add 'instant jungle' to a room. Its large, deep green heart-shaped leaves are covered with holes and splits, making it a real statement plant. It's a climber and its stems can be trained up a support (where it will attach roots) or left to trail. Its sheer size makes monstera a great plant for filling a bright corner of a room. Another monstera to look out for is *Monstera adansonii*, a much more compact plant that has smaller leaves with larger holes and looks fantastic trailing out of a hanging basket.

HOW TO GROW:

1. Depending on the size of your plant, choose a pot around 5cm wider and taller than its current pot, with good drainage holes. The larger the pot, the larger the plant will grow, so consider this when choosing a pot.
2. Position the pot in a brightly lit spot indoors that doesn't receive direct sunlight.
3. Half fill the pot with a quality potting mix, such as Yates Premium Potting Mix. It's a good idea to place a support post in the pot when you're filling it with potting mix, so it's ready to train the monstera up as it grows.
4. Remove the monstera from its container, position in the new pot and gently backfill with potting mix. The level of the potting mix should be the same as the original level of mix around the plant, so all the roots are covered.
5. Water well to settle the potting mix around the roots.
6. Monsteras like to be kept only slightly moist. Check moisture levels by inserting your finger into the top few centimetres of mix. If it feels dry, water the plant; if it's still moist, leave watering for a few days.
7. To promote healthy foliage growth, from spring to autumn feed once a month with Yates Thrive All Purpose Liquid Plant Food.

GROWING TIPS:

- Gently dust the leaves regularly to keep them clean and healthy.
- They don't grow very quickly, so can stay in the same pot for several years.
- Monsteras will enjoy having their foliage misted with water during hot dry weather.
- If the plant becomes too large, the stems can be trimmed and used as cuttings to create more plants.

44

- Yates Premium Potting Mix
- Yates Thrive All Purpose Liquid Plant Food

UMBRELLA TREE
Schefflera actinophylla

Umbrella or octopus trees can develop into sizeable indoor plants, with multiple glossy green leaves that grow in clusters from stem tips, creating a bold tropical statement in the corner of a room or against a wall. They're robust, low maintenance plants that are ideal for people who can't devote too much time to caring for their indoor plants, but still want lots of greenery. Umbrella trees will grow to around 2m tall indoors and look fabulous both on their own or grouped together with other plants.

HOW TO GROW:

1. Depending on the size of your plant, choose a pot around 5cm wider and taller than its current pot, with good drainage holes. The larger the pot, the larger the plant will grow, so consider this when choosing a pot.
2. Position the pot in a brightly lit spot indoors that doesn't receive direct sunlight and is protected from draughts.
3. Half fill the pot with a quality potting mix, such as Yates Premium Potting Mix.
4. Carefully remove the umbrella tree from its container. Position in the new pot and gently backfill with potting mix. The level of the potting mix should be the same as the original level of mix around the plant, so all the roots are covered.
5. Water well to settle the potting mix around the roots.
6. Allow the top few centimetres of potting mix to dry out before re-watering. Check moisture levels by inserting your finger into the top few centimetres of mix. If it feels dry, water the plant; if it's still moist, leave watering for a few days.
7. To promote lush healthy foliage growth, from spring to autumn feed every month with Yates Thrive All Purpose Liquid Plant Food.

GROWING TIPS:

- Umbrella trees can drop their leaves if moved, so avoid moving this plant unless necessary.
- To keep the plant at a manageable height or to promote bushier growth, the tips of the stems can be pruned or the plant cut back by a third.
- Don't be tempted to plant an umbrella tree outside. In some areas they're classified as weeds and can become invasive.

45

RECOMMENDED PRODUCTS:

- Yates Premium Potting Mix
- Yates Thrive All Purpose Liquid Plant Food

WAFFLE PLANT

Hemigraphis spp.

Waffle or red ivy plants are compact and colourful plants with rich burgundy and green dimpled foliage. Only growing to around 20cm tall, they're an ideal vibrant plant for a table top, office desk or shelf. They will also enjoy growing in a brightly lit, humid bathroom or under a decorative glass dome. They can also spread horizontally and be grown in a hanging basket where their beautiful purple foliage and stems can drape over the sides.

HOW TO GROW:

1. Choose a pot at least 20cm wide that has good drainage holes.
2. Position the pot in a brightly lit spot indoors that doesn't receive direct sunlight.
3. Half fill the pot with a quality potting mix, such as Yates Premium Potting Mix.
4. Remove the waffle plant from its container, position in the new pot and gently backfill with potting mix. The level of the potting mix should be the same as the original level of mix around the plant, so all the roots are covered but not any of the leaves.
5. Water well to settle the potting mix around the roots.
6. Keep the potting mix consistently slightly moist. Check moisture levels by inserting your finger into the top few centimetres of mix. If it feels dry, water the plant; if it's still moist, leave watering for a few days.
7. To promote healthy colourful foliage growth, from spring to autumn feed every month with Yates Thrive All Purpose Liquid Plant Food.

GROWING TIPS:

- Waffle plants love humidity so their foliage can be misted regularly with water, particularly during hot dry weather, or place their pot on a saucer of water that's filled with pebbles and regularly add water to the saucer.
- Remove any dead leaves to keep the plant looking tidy and trim back stems to help keep the plant bushier and more compact.
- Propagate more waffle plants by inserting 10cm lengths of stem that contain a node (a bump on the stem) into moist potting mix and roots will develop in a few weeks.

46

WATERMELON PEPEROMIA

Peperomia argyreia

Watermelon peperomia is another must-have indoor plant. Its silvery white striped leaves are similar to the patterns on watermelon skin, hence their name. They're hardy, compact plants that don't get larger than 30cm tall and wide, so they are a great choice for small spaces like shelves and table tops. Their beautiful foliage makes them a fabulous feature plant all on their own; however, they look just as eye catching when grown among other indoor plants with complementary patterned or completely contrasting foliage.

RECOMMENDED PRODUCTS:

• Yates Premium Potting Mix

• Yates Thrive All Purpose
. Liquid Plant Food

HOW TO GROW:

1. Choose a pot at least 15cm wide, or slightly larger than the existing pot, that has good drainage holes.
2. Position the pot in a brightly lit spot indoors that doesn't receive direct sunlight.
3. Half fill the pot with a quality potting mix, such as Yates Premium Potting Mix.
4. Remove the watermelon peperomia from its container, position in the new pot and gently backfill with potting mix. The level of the potting mix should be the same as the original level of mix around the plant, so all the roots are covered but not any of the leaves.
5. Water well to settle the potting mix around the roots.
6. Keep the potting mix slightly moist. Check moisture levels by inserting your finger into the top few centimetres of mix. If it feels dry, water the plant; if it's still moist, leave watering for a few days. Peperomias don't like to be waterlogged.
7. To promote healthy foliage growth, from spring to autumn feed every month with Yates Thrive All Purpose Liquid Plant Food.

GROWING TIPS:

• Watermelon peperomias can be left in the same pot for a few years.
• Remove any dead leaves to keep the plant looking tidy.
• To create new plants, cut off a healthy leaf together with 3cm of stem and insert the stem into moist potting mix so that the bottom of the leaf is just touching the mix. Keep the mix moist and once roots form, the baby plants can be potted into their own pots.

47

WEEPING FIG

Ficus benjamina

Weeping figs have featured in living rooms for many years and bring an instant jungle feel indoors. They can grow into tall plants with masses of leaves and create a striking indoor focal point. Weeping figs can have dark lush green or variegated foliage from top to pot or be trained or woven into a very decorative standard (ball-on-a-stick or lollipop style).

HOW TO GROW:

1. Depending on the size of your plant, choose a pot around 5cm wider and taller than its current pot, with good drainage holes.
2. Position the pot in a brightly lit spot indoors. It will tolerate some direct morning sunlight but not harsh midday or afternoon sun.
3. Half fill the pot with a quality potting mix, such as Yates Premium Potting Mix.
4. Carefully remove the weeping fig from its container. Position in the new pot and gently backfill with potting mix. The level of the potting mix should be the same as the original level of mix around the plant, so all the roots are covered.
5. Water well to settle the potting mix around the roots.
6. Keep the potting mix consistently slightly moist. Check moisture levels by inserting your finger into the top few centimetres of mix. If it feels dry, water the plant; if it's still moist, leave watering for a few days.
7. To promote lush healthy foliage growth, from spring to autumn feed every 2 weeks with Yates Thrive All Purpose Liquid Plant Food.

GROWING TIPS:

•   Avoid moving weeping figs, as a change in environment can cause the leaves to drop.
•   During hot dry weather, weeping figs will appreciate their foliage being misted with water.
•   It's best to leave weeping figs in the same pot for several years as they resent disturbance.
•   Don't be tempted to plant a weeping fig in the ground in suburban areas as their root systems can be very invasive.

48

RECOMMENDED PRODUCTS:

• Yates Thrive Houseplant
Liquid Plant Food

ZEBRA CACTUS

Haworthia fasciata

Although called a cactus, this is a very attractive clump-forming succulent native to South Africa, with striking horizontal white stripes around its pointed leaves. Perfect for growing indoors, zebra cactus is a small, slow growing, low maintenance succulent that is ideal for office desks and looks fantastic when planted in a shallow glass dish with layers of decorative gravel.

HOW TO GROW:

1. Choose a pot around 10cm wide that has good drainage holes.
2. Position the pot in a brightly lit spot indoors. It will tolerate some direct morning sunlight.
3. Half fill the pot with a quality, free draining cacti and succulent potting mix.
4. Remove the zebra cactus from its container, position in the new pot and gently backfill with potting mix. The level of the potting mix should be the same as the original level of mix around the plant, so all the roots are covered but not any of the leaves.
5. Water well to settle the potting mix around the roots.
6. Keep the potting mix only slightly moist. Check moisture levels by inserting your finger into the top few centimetres of mix. If it feels dry, water the plant; if it's still moist, leave watering for a few days. Watering can be reduced during the cooler months. Zebra cactus does not like to be overwatered.
7. To promote healthy growth, from spring to autumn feed every month with Yates Thrive Houseplant Liquid Plant Food.

GROWING TIPS:

• Due to their slow growth, zebra cactus will live quite happily for many years in the same pot.
• Zebra cactus may produce baby plants around the base, which can be carefully separated and planted into their own pot.
• Don't allow zebra cactus to sit in a saucer of water, which can lead to leaf and root rot.

49

ZEBRA PLANT

Aphelandra squarrosa

Native to Brazil, zebra plants are aptly named, having large deep green leaves with dramatic white veins. Growing to between 30 and 60cm tall, they can sometimes also produce showy bright yellow flowers which can last for many weeks. Zebra plants can be a bit temperamental about light, water and humidity levels and shouldn't be the first choice for beginner gardeners; however, their exotic jungle appearance makes them well worth ultimately including in your indoor plant collection.

RECOMMENDED PRODUCTS:

- Yates Premium Potting Mix
- Yates Thrive Houseplant Liquid Plant Food

HOW TO GROW:

1. Depending on the size of your zebra plant, choose a pot at least 20cm wide that has good drainage holes.
2. Position the pot in a warm, brightly lit spot indoors that doesn't receive direct sunlight and is protected from cold draughts.
3. Half fill the pot with a quality potting mix, such as Yates Premium Potting Mix.
4. Remove the zebra plant from its container, position in the new pot and gently backfill with potting mix. The level of the potting mix should be the same as the original level of mix around the plant, so all the roots are covered.
5. Water well to settle the potting mix around the roots.
6. Keep the potting mix consistently moist. Check moisture levels by inserting your finger into the top few centimetres of mix. If it feels dry, water the plant; if it's still moist, leave watering for a few days.
7. Zebra plants require lots of feeding, and to promote healthy colourful foliage growth, from spring to autumn feed every fortnight with Yates Thrive Houseplant Liquid Plant Food.

GROWING TIPS:

- Cut off spent flowers. To help keep the plant bushy and compact, stems can be trimmed back.
- They don't mind becoming slightly pot bound and can stay in the same pot for several years.
- Zebra plants love humidity and will enjoy having their foliage misted with water during hot dry weather; you can also sit the pot on a saucer of water that's filled with pebbles and regularly add water to the saucer.
- Zebra plants can be propagated by taking 10cm stem cuttings and inserting them in moist potting mix.

50

RECOMMENDED PRODUCTS:

- Yates Premium Potting Mix
- Yates Thrive All Purpose Liquid Plant Food

ZZ PLANT

Zamioculcas zamiifolia

You could be forgiven for thinking that the ZZ plant, also called Zanzibar Gem, is artificial. It has wonderfully shiny, thick waxy deep green leaves and stems and the plant has a fascinating prehistoric appearance. It's a very tough, slow growing plant that will survive in low light and with minimal watering and feeding, making it a perfect choice for office environments and time-poor indoor gardeners. ZZ plants eventually grow to around 60–90cm tall and have an upright growth habit, so they don't take up too much horizontal space. These plants look fantastic when planted into crisp white pots or troughs.

HOW TO GROW:

1. A ZZ plant will be happy in the same pot for several years; however, if it needs re-potting, depending on the size of your plant, choose a pot around 5cm wider and taller than its current pot, with good drainage holes.
2. Position the pot in a brightly lit spot indoors that does not receive direct sunlight. ZZ plants will also tolerate more dimly lit positions.
3. Half fill the pot with a quality, free draining potting mix like Yates Premium Potting Mix.
4. Remove the ZZ plant from its container, position in the new pot and gently backfill with potting mix. The level of the potting mix should be the same as the original level of mix around the plant, so all the roots are covered.
5. Water well to settle the potting mix around the roots.
6. ZZ plants should be allowed to dry out in between waterings. Check moisture levels by inserting your finger into the top few centimetres of mix. If it feels dry, water the plant; if it's still moist, leave watering for a few days. Watering can be reduced during the cooler months. They do not like to be overwatered.
7. To promote healthy growth, from spring to autumn feed every month with half strength Yates Thrive All Purpose Liquid Plant Food.

GROWING TIPS:

- Keep the leaves clean by gently wiping with a damp cloth.
- During hot dry weather their foliage can be misted with water.

INDOOR PLANT CARE

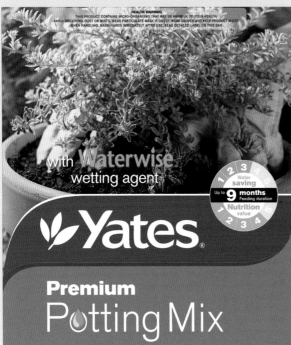

with **Waterwise** wetting agent

Water saving

Up to **9 months** Feeding duration

Nutrition value

🌿 **Yates**®

Premium Potting Mix

Now that you have a brand-new indoor plant or are wondering how to keep your current indoor plant family looking lush and fabulous, here is some simple plant care information and tips.

TYPES OF POTTING MIX

There is a myriad of different types and grades of potting mixes available. Modern day potting mixes have been designed to be suitable for growing potted plants. Most contain a mixture of composted pinebark, sand and plant fertilisers, and some contain additives like wetting agents, water-absorbent crystals and beneficial microorganisms. Don't be tempted to dig up soil from your garden and use it for your potted plants. It will be the quickest way to kill your new leafy friend!

With potting mixes you really do get what you pay for. Cheap potting mixes may not have the correct structural or nutritional qualities, resulting in poor plant growth. It's well worth using the best quality potting mix you can afford, such as Yates Premium Potting Mix.

It's a good idea to use specialist potting mixes for plants like orchids, cacti and succulents. They have been developed to provide the best growing environment for those plants. For orchids the mix should be very coarse and allow water to easily drain away, and for cacti and succulents the mix should also be free-draining.

Some potting mixes will contain slow-release nutrients that will feed the plant during its early months. Check the label of your chosen potting mix to see whether it contains additional nutrients and when it is recommended to start supplemental feeding.

TYPES OF POTS

Pots have come a wonderfully long way in colour and design since the fairly plain, earthy green and brown pots of the 1970s and delightful folk-art decorations of the 1980s. (However, there is now quite a demand for these retro-look pots.) The range of fabulous and decorative pots now available is dizzying and a pot is sometimes what a person falls in love with first, with the plant choice coming second.

The main types of pots are made from terracotta, plastic, ceramics, fibreglass, concrete or lightweight blended materials. The choice of which type of pot to use needs to be based on several things, including where inside the plant will be growing, where you live (will you have to lug a heavy concrete pot up multiple flights of stairs?), the type and size of your plants, your interior design and personal choice and budget.

When you're purchasing plants and pots, it's a great idea to bring the two together, before you leave the garden centre, and see what the combination looks like. For example, upright mother-in-law's tongue makes a fantastic statement in tall narrow pots, and smaller leafy plants like peperomia and polka dot plants look wonderful in a bowl.

Rustic looking terracotta pots, which are usually relatively cheap, are porous and can lose moisture through the pot walls, so tend to dry out faster than other types of pots. This more rapid drying can suit plants which detest wet feet, such as the Chinese money plant (*Pilea peperomioides*), succulents and bromeliads. Plastic pots are lightweight, cheap, long lasting, don't lose moisture through their walls and are ideal where weight could be an issue (such as hanging baskets); however, many are not particularly decorative. Ceramic pots are available in almost every gorgeous colour and design and can look very impressive but they are also heavy and may be expensive. Fibreglass and lightweight pots also come in a wide range of beautiful colours and shapes and their reduced weight makes them easier to use and move around inside homes.

Whichever pot you choose, make sure it has adequate drainage holes. The quickest way to kill an indoor plant is to drown it in a poorly drained pot. Some decorative pots don't have drainage holes and

unless you want to risk drilling holes in the base, which may damage or crack the pot, the easiest way to overcome this is to keep the plant in a slightly smaller plain plastic pot and sit it inside the decorative pot. It's important to not let the bottom of the decorative pot fill up with water, which will rot the plant roots. The additional benefit of 'hiding' a plain plastic pot inside a decorative one is that you can easily swap plants around as they grow, or create a whole new look with the same plant in a different pot. If you want to disguise the top of the plastic pot, you can use a layer of coconut fibre, which is lightweight and easy to apply and remove when required.

Many pots will come with or have a matching saucer available. If you want a saucer, a tip is to buy the pot and saucer at the same time, so you can check their sizes together and match their colours before you leave the store. Saucers are particularly handy for indoor gardening as they help to reduce water leaking and potting mix spilling onto carpets, flooring and furniture. Even when using saucers, it's still important after watering to monitor whether any water secretly overflows from the saucer. Carpets, timber floors and furniture can be very unforgiving if exposed to constant moisture. Also be mindful of pots marking surfaces, either through sheer weight or by creating scratches.

Unless you're going away on holidays for a few days or the weather is very warm, water should not be left in saucers. It creates a permanently soggy zone of potting mix at the base of the pot, which leads to the potting mix and roots starting to rot. You may also start to smell a rotten egg type odour. So, after you've finished watering a plant, tip out any water that has soaked into the saucer. If the pot is too heavy to lift, extra water can be soaked up from the saucer using an old towel.

Consider the size of your pot in relation to the size of the plant. Although it's tempting, avoid planting into a pot that is significantly bigger than your plant. If you put a small plant in a big pot, an unhealthy environment can be created around the roots and plant health can suffer. Where possible, it's better to gradually increase the size of the pot as the plant grows. Also think about the scale of your plant in relation to the size of the pot. A tall plant in a shallow pot is more likely to tip over and will look out of place. For the best effect, match the pot with the dimensions of the plant. If you're still unsure, an easy rule of thumb for upright leafy plants is two 'parts' plant height to one 'part' plant pot height.

Self-watering pots have a water reservoir at their base which plants can draw upon as they need moisture. They are a great choice for beginner gardeners as they take some of the guesswork out of watering – just keep the water reservoir topped up.

Hanging baskets are wonderful for making use of vertical spaces and showing off plants with a cascading or trailing habit. Like other pots, hanging baskets are made from all different types of materials, including plastic, ceramics and metal, and can come with attached wires or hangers, or you can support standard pots in super trendy macramé hangers. Hanging baskets can dry out faster than pots placed on the floor, as they are exposed to greater airflow and draughts, so it's important to check potting mix moisture levels regularly. Hanging baskets are also available with water reservoirs, which help to extend the watering interval.

Vertical gardens are the ultimate space saver, taking up very little horizontal floor or furniture space, and can create a beautiful living green wall. There's a multitude of different styles, designs and sizes of vertical gardens including upright stands or frames with room for multiple pots, troughs or pockets, and standalone wall units with inbuilt irrigation systems (some including a fish tank at the bottom!). Vertical gardens are designed to be closely planted, the result being a lush wall of greenery. Even a small vertical garden is a very soothing addition to indoor spaces. Monitor potting mix moisture levels regularly in vertical garden systems, as plants are usually growing in a limited volume of potting mix and can run out of water quickly.

Plants in self-watering pots draw water from the reservoir at the base as they need it.

HOW TO POT UP AN INDOOR PLANT

When you buy an indoor plant, whether an irresistible new pot comes home with it or you already have the 'perfect pot' at home, the next step is to plant it into the new container.

Here are the easy how-to steps for potting up most indoor plants:

- The chosen pot should not be significantly bigger than your new plant. It's tempting to buy a big pot and think that it will reduce the number of times you'll have to re-pot as the plant grows. However, a small plant growing in a big pot will become unhealthy. It's better to upsize gradually.
- If it's a heavy pot, it's best to place the pot in its final location before filling with any potting mix, which will only make it heavier.
- Partially fill the pot with good quality potting mix. Choose a specialist potting mix for particular plant types. For example, for African violets use an open, light and well-drained African violet mix.
- Remove the plant from its current pot. If the roots are tangled and dense, it's a good idea to gently tease apart some of the outer roots to help encourage fresh growth. The exception to this is palms, which don't like their roots being disturbed.
- Position the plant in the new pot and gently backfill around it with potting mix. The level of the potting mix should be the same as the original level of mix around the plant, so all the roots are covered but none of the leaves or stems.
- Water well to settle the potting mix around the roots and eliminate large air pockets.

If you have an indoor plant that's beginning to outgrow its existing container, or it's been in the same pot for a long time and the potting mix has aged and shrunk, it's time to do a refresh. The best time to do this is from spring to early autumn, when the weather is warm enough to encourage fresh root and leaf growth. When you need to use the same pot, rather than progressing to a larger pot, here are the steps to giving your plant a new lease on life:

• Give the plant a good water a few hours before re-potting.
• Gently remove the plant from its existing pot. This may require the removal of any roots that have grown through the drainage holes and some careful tapping, wriggling and coaxing.
• If the plant has become pot-bound or the roots have become tangled and filled the pot, you can carefully cut away up to a third of the root ball. Now is also a good opportunity to divide congested clumps of plants like mother-in-law's tongue, spider plants, peace lily and cast iron plant to create new ones.
• Place the root-trimmed plant back in the pot and backfill with fresh potting mix. The level of the potting mix should be the same as the original level of mix around the plant, so all the roots are covered.
• Water the plant well to settle the potting mix around the root ball.
• Keep the plant well watered as it recovers from the stress of re-potting. You can start feeding the plant once new stems and leaves begin to emerge.
• Avoid removing or disturbing palm roots, as they resent any root disturbance.

HOW TO WATER

Overwatering and underwatering are two of the biggest killers of indoor plants. We either waterlog them to death or they die of dehydration.

The plant profiles contained in this book give watering guidelines for each plant. Some plants prefer to be kept on the drier side; other plants do best when their potting mix is kept moist. Adjusting watering levels to suit your plant is the first important step in keeping it happy and healthy. One of the easiest ways to check moisture levels in potting mix is with your finger. Insert your finger into the top few centimetres of mix. You will be able to feel whether it's still moist or whether it feels dry and dusty.

Don't leave water in pot saucers. This creates a constantly wet layer of potting mix on the bottom of the pot, which can lead to roots rotting and the potting mix anaerobically decomposing (which can smell like rotten eggs).

If your watering routine is less than perfect then consider using a self-watering pot, which is a pot that contains a special water-holding reservoir in the base. Plants can draw on this water over several days as they need it.

When potting mix dries out completely, it can be hard to re-wet. Potting mix may shrink away from the pot wall and when the plant is watered, water may seep in between the pot wall and the edge of the potting mix and not penetrate into the root ball of the plant, even though the saucer may fill with water. If this happens, you can help thoroughly re-wet the potting mix by applying a soil wetting agent, such as Yates Waterwise Soil Wetter, over the surface of the potting mix. This helps to break down the waxy, water repellent layer on the potting mix and enable moisture to move more evenly and effectively down into the root zone. This can be reapplied several times a year. Alternatively, the pot (which must have drainage holes) can be almost fully submerged in a sink or bucket of water. The water level in the sink should be below the rim of the pot, otherwise potting mix can float off the surface. Leave the pot for around 20 minutes to allow the root zone and all the potting mix to become thoroughly wet. The water will seep in through the drainage holes at the bottom of the pot and up into the potting mix. After the 20 minutes is up, remove the pot from the water and allow it to drain before putting it back on its saucer.

Getting your watering technique right can also assist with reducing the incidence of diseases. Disease spores can be splashed from the potting mix up onto the foliage, so watering the potting mix gently can help minimise this. For many plants, damp foliage, particularly overnight, can increase the risk of disease. Watering in the morning allows foliage to dry out during the day, helping to reduce the chance of disease. A small watering can with a narrow spout, rather than a large rose, is ideal for watering indoor plants, as you can direct the water onto the potting mix rather than over the foliage.

For plants that don't mind getting their leaves wet, you can put them in the shower recess and give them a gentle shower with tepid water. This has the added benefit of washing any dust off leaves at the same time. Give your plants a shower in the morning, which allows the foliage a chance to dry off during the day. Alternatively, you can take indoor plants outside, into a very sheltered and shady part of a garden, patio or balcony, and give them a gentle hose. It's crucial that they're not in direct sunlight or a windy spot, which will damage their leaves. Move them back inside as soon as the foliage has dried.

If you're going away and have to leave your indoor plants for a few days, here are a few options to help keep them at their well-watered leafy best until you return:

- Water all your plants thoroughly before you go. Many plants will survive for quite a few days without being watered, particularly during cool weather.
- Ask a neighbour to come and water your plants for you. You could repay the favour and water their plants when they go away, or fellow plant enthusiasts will always appreciate a thank you gift of a cutting or a new plant.
- For small or medium sized plants, put a plug in the laundry tub or bath tub, place an old towel in the bottom of the tub, thoroughly wet the towel and place your plants (without their saucers) on the towel. The wet towel acts as a moisture reservoir over a few days. Ensure that your tap is completely off, so that the tub doesn't fill with water.
- Potted plants, with saucers removed, can also be moved into the shower recess and placed on an old wet towel.

Watering can usually be decreased over the cool months, as plant growth slows down and air temperatures drop. Continue to monitor potting mix moisture levels during winter to determine when you need to water, as plants will still need some moisture to survive.

HUMIDITY

Many indoor plants are native to tropical rainforests, so love humidity. Bathrooms and kitchens can be the steamiest rooms in the house, so humidity-loving plants are ideally suited to those spaces. However, summer air conditioning and winter heating can really dry out the air, making it challenging for indoor plants to thrive, so use the following tricks with your humidity-loving indoor plants:

- Regularly mist the foliage with tepid water using a plastic spray bottle, particularly during hot dry weather. Do this during the morning to allow the foliage to dry off during the day.
- Place a layer of pebbles or marbles in a saucer, add water so it's almost covering the pebbles, then put the pot on the pebbles. This helps create a more humid environment around the plant, but doesn't allow roots to sit in water. In hot dry weather you'll need to top up the water more often.
- For dedicated growers, consider using an electric room humidifier during very dry weather.

HOW TO FEED

Potted plants are completely reliant on us for their nutrition. The nutrients in potting mix will only last a limited time and after that the plants will need regular feeding to help keep them happy and healthy. Well-fed plants will have more lush and healthy leaves, and flowering plants will produce more blooms. Well-fed plants will also be more resistant to attack from pests and diseases.

There are different types of fertilisers that are suitable for feeding indoor plants. These include liquids, pellets, prills and granules, which can be made from synthetic ingredients, organic materials or a combination of both.

- Liquid plant foods – liquid formulations, usually containing fast-acting nutrients, which are mixed with water before being applied over the potting mix. Liquid fertilisers provide plants with an instant feed and have to be reapplied on a regular basis.
- Pelletised plant foods – these are commonly based on organic materials like manure; some are fortified with additional nutrients. Organic based fertilisers release nutrients slowly to the plant over several weeks or months as they break down and add beneficial organic matter to the potting mix; they also encourage beneficial soil microorganisms.
- Prilled plant foods – these are small granules of compressed fertiliser that can be coated with a barrier to slow down the release of nutrients (often referred to as controlled release fertilisers). They're sprinkled over the surface of the potting mix and release nutrients to the plant slowly over many weeks or months.
- Granular plant foods – these are granules of concentrated nutrients that are best suited to outdoor garden beds, as they are usually too strong for use on potted plants.

Plants require three main nutrients for healthy growth: nitrogen (N), which promotes green leaf growth; phosphorus (P), which encourages strong root development; and potassium (K), which helps flowering and also healthy plant growth. A fertiliser that contains these three nutrients is called a 'complete' plant food. It's important to feed indoor plants with complete plant foods to ensure they receive all the nutrients they require for lush healthy growth.

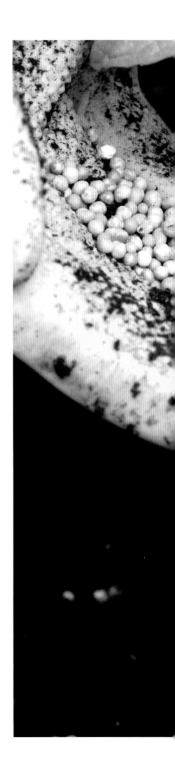

Some plants do best with specially developed complete plant foods, which contain the right balance of nitrogen, phosphorus and potassium to bring out their special attributes. For example, flowering indoor plants should be fed with a potassium-enriched plant food, such as Yates Thrive Roses & Flowers Liquid Plant Food, to promote lots of beautiful flowers.

Unless indoor plants are growing or flowering during the cooler months, it's best to only feed from spring to autumn, while the weather is warm enough for plant growth. Give them a break from feeding during winter.

Whichever fertiliser you choose, always follow the dilution and reapplication directions on the label.

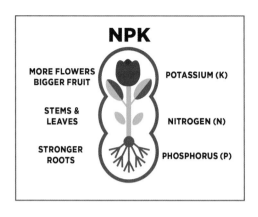

NPK

MORE FLOWERS
BIGGER FRUIT — POTASSIUM (K)

STEMS &
LEAVES — NITROGEN (N)

STRONGER
ROOTS — PHOSPHORUS (P)

LEFT: The leaf on this plant is showing evidence of nutrient deprivation.

SUNLIGHT

The amount of sun that streams into an indoor space is one of the main factors that can determine whether your indoor plants will flourish or not. Your plants will not grow in the dark! If your light levels are less than ideal, there are some indoor plants that will grow quite happily in low levels of light or that tolerate fluorescent lighting in windowless offices, such as mother-in-law's tongue, peace lily, Chinese evergreen, devil's ivy and cast iron plant.

Most indoor plants will do best where they receive bright but indirect light. Direct sunlight can burn or scorch the leaves of many indoor plants or cause leaves to yellow. A plant that prefers a brightly lit spot will develop long and lanky growth in a dark room and be generally unhappy. If plants start to 'lean' towards a window, that can be an indicator that they would like more light.

Some indoor plants, particularly taller growing plants like Japanese aralia, rubber plant, China doll, fiddle leaf fig and philodrendron, will benefit from having their pots rotated by 90 degrees every week or so. This allows all sides of the foliage to receive the brightest light and encourages more even, less lopsided growth. Use caution when rotating plants like weeping figs, which can sulk and drop their leaves if they're moved.

Be mindful of how the amount of sunlight entering a room can vary across the year. For example, during winter when the sun is lower in the sky, more sunlight may come into a room for a longer period of time compared to summer, when the sun is higher in the sky. You may need to move plants to a different spot in the room or house so that they're protected from direct sunlight. If this isn't possible, consider hanging a sheer curtain in front of the window to filter the sunlight.

Monitor the heat that might come through a window, even if there's no direct sunlight. Elevated temperatures can rapidly dry out potting mix and result in plants wilting and leaf damage. Also take care if warmth-loving plants are near windows during the cooler months. Uncovered windows are not particularly effective insulators against the cold and tender indoor plants can suffer from damage during cold or frosty nights.

Some indoor plants do enjoy or tolerate some direct sunlight, with gentler morning sun being the best. Plants like zebra cactus, chain of hearts and weeping figs can be grown in rooms that get some direct morning sun, but should be protected from strong midday and afternoon sun.

Most newly purchased plants will include a label that contains some helpful information about the amount of light that your new plant prefers, so check the label for additional guidance.

PESTS

There are usually no natural predators for insects affecting indoor plants, so without intervention, numbers can increase rapidly. Pests can be easily kept in check once you know what early symptoms to look for, work out which pest you're dealing with and then choose the appropriate control method.

Here are the most common pests that occur on indoor plants:

- Mealybugs – sap-sucking insect pests that can be common on indoor plants like palms, dracaena and orchids. They are around 3mm long and are covered in a white furry coating, which sometimes appears hairy. Mealybugs are often found on the lower stems of plants, hiding in among leaf bases. They excrete a sweet sticky substance called honeydew, which can attract ants and a fungal disease called sooty mould. Sooty mould appears as a dark grey or black ash-like coating over leaves and stems. In addition to attracting sooty mould, mealybugs deplete plants of valuable nutrients and sugars and adversely affect plant health.
- Spider mites – sometimes called two spotted or red spider mites, these are tiny sap-sucking pests. Less than 1mm long, they're very difficult to see with the naked eye. The first noticeable symptom is usually yellowing or mottled foliage, and when spider mite colonies increase, they will form spidery webbing in between leaves. Mites like hot dry weather, so are more common during summer. Mite infestations damage plant health and can cause plants to die if left untreated.
- Aphids – small insects that suck the sap from plants. Aphids are about 2mm long and can be black, grey, yellow, green or brown. They are particularly attracted to soft new growth, but can also infest older leaves and stems, and can breed very rapidly. Affected leaves can curl and distort and plant health can suffer. Like mealybugs, aphids excrete honeydew, which can attract ants and sooty mould.
- Scale – sap-sucking insects that hide under a hard, soft or furry waxy coating that can be white, grey, brown or black. They're around 3–5mm long and can attack both leaves and stems. Scale insects on leaves can cause a corresponding yellow spot on the opposite leaf surface and plant growth can slow down as the insects remove important sugars and nutrients from the plant. Like aphids, scale produce honeydew, which attracts ants and sooty mould.

- Fungus gnats – often mistakenly called 'fruit flies', fungus gnats are tiny black winged insects, around 3mm long, which can live in and around moist potting mix. Their larvae feed on organic matter and large populations can damage plant roots, leading to wilted and sick plants.
- Whitefly – tiny white flying insects that are around 1–2mm long. They breed rapidly and will often fly up in a cloud when disturbed. They suck the sap from plants, causing plant health to decline, and excrete honeydew, which attracts sooty mould.
- Thrips – tiny insects 0.5–1.5mm long which feed on plant juices and can cause leaves and flowers to distort and discolour.
- Caterpillars – chewing insects that can eat holes in leaves, stems and also flowers. Caterpillars can come in varying colours and sizes, from green or brown to spotted or hairy. Caterpillars are often camouflaged and hard to find, with their damage or droppings being the first things that will be noticed.

ABOVE: Mealybugs
RIGHT: Mites

Small numbers of pests can be gently scraped away, picked off or squished. However, larger infestations may need to be controlled with sprays.

PEST	SOLUTION
Aphids Spider mites Whitefly	Yates Nature's Way Vegie & Herb Spray (Natrasoap)* (Aust. only) Yates Nature's Way Natrasoap Vegie Insect Gun* (NZ only)
Mealybug Thrips	Yates Nature's Way Vegie & Herb Spray (Natrasoap)* (Aust. only) Yates Nature's Way Organic Citrus, Vegie & Ornamental Spray** (NZ only)
Scale Caterpillars	Yates Nature's Way Citrus & Ornamental Spray** (Aust. only) Yates Nature's Way Organic Citrus, Vegie & Ornamental Spray** (NZ only)
Fungus gnats	Hang yellow sticky traps near affected plants, reduce watering to allow the top layer of potting mix to dry out, apply a layer of sand or small pebbles over the top of the potting mix to deter female fungus gnats from laying their eggs.

*An insecticidal soap made from natural vegetable oils. It's certified for use in organic gardening.

**Based on natural pyrethrin from the pyrethrum daisy, and vegetable oil, and contains added seaweed to boost plant growth. It's certified for use in organic gardening.

TOP LEFT: Aphids
TOP RIGHT: White fly
MID LEFT: Thrips
MID RIGHT: Fungus gnats
BOTTOM LEFT: Scale
BOTTOM RIGHT: Caterpillar

DISEASES

Plant diseases can be exacerbated by the moist protected environments found indoors, particularly when we love growing lots of plants in close jungle-like proximity! The chance of disease can be reduced by growing plants in their preferred location, such as in a dry, airy or brightly lit spot versus an area with high humidity. Correct watering techniques can also help to reduce disease. Disease spores can be splashed from the potting mix up onto the foliage, so carefully and gently watering the potting mix can help minimise this. For many plants, damp foliage, particularly overnight, can also increase the risk of disease. Watering in the morning allows foliage to dry out during the day, reducing the risk of disease. As soon as any disease symptoms are noticed, remove the affected leaf or leaves to help prevent the spread to healthy foliage.

Despite our best efforts, diseases can still occur. The most common diseases on indoor plants include:

- Powdery mildew – a fungal disease that is favoured by warm, humid conditions and appears as spots of white or grey coloured ash over leaves and stems, which can eventually cover large areas of the plant. Affected leaves can turn yellow and develop brown or dead patches.
- Downy mildew – a disease that appears as tufty grey patches underneath leaves with corresponding dark markings on the upper surface of the leaf. Downy mildew can result in dying and dead spots on foliage.
- Leaf spots – brown or black spots that can develop into holes and spread to cover large areas of the leaves.
- Botrytis (grey mould) – a fluffy mould growth that often starts on old or dead foliage and stems and can spread to other parts of the plant including leaves, stems and flowers. Botrytis can also cause plants to wilt and leaves to yellow or flower petals develop spots.
- Root rot – plants with root rot disease will often start to wilt, due to their inability to absorb sufficient moisture. Wilting foliage caused by root rot may be confused with dehydrated plants due to underwatering, so it's important to check soil moisture levels.
- Rust – orange, yellow or reddish pustules on leaves or stems that have a corresponding yellow spot on the other side of the leaf.
- Sooty mould – a disease that looks like a black ash covering leaves and stems. Sooty mould disease grows on the sweet sticky honeydew that is excreted by sap-sucking insects like aphids, scale and mealybugs. Once the insects are controlled, the sooty mould will disappear.

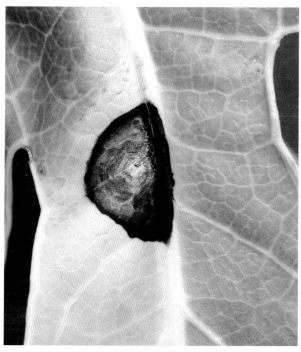

TOP LEFT: Powdery mildew
TOP RIGHT: Downy mildew
LEFT: Leaf spot
ABOVE: Botrytis

TOP LEFT: Root rot
TOP RIGHT: Sooty mould
LEFT: Rust

DISEASE	SOLUTION
Powdery mildew	Yates Rose Gun, Yates Fungus Gun, Yates Nature's Way Fungus Spray (NZ only)
Downy mildew	Yates Liquid Copper Fungicide, Yates Nature's Way Fungus Spray (NZ only)
Leaf spots	Yates Liquid Copper Fungicide, Yates Leaf Curl Fungicide (Aust. only), Yates Copper Oxychloride Fungicide (NZ only)
Botrytis (grey mould)	Remove and destroy infected foliage, reduce levels of humidity, don't water or mist foliage, improve airflow.
Root rot	Improve drainage and / or reduce watering. Yates Anti Rot Phosacid Systemic Fungicide (Aust. only)
Sooty mould	Control sucking insects with Yates Nature's Way Citrus & Ornamental Spray (Aust. only) Yates Nature's Way Organic Citrus, Vegie & Ornamental Spray (NZ only)
Rust	Yates Rose Gun, Yates Fungus Gun

It's important to ensure thorough coverage and spray both sides of foliage. Always use sprays as per the label and safety directions. Where possible, it's a good idea to move indoor plants to a very shady and sheltered spot outdoors before spraying them. This prevents sprays from contacting furniture and other household surfaces. Move the plant back indoors once the spray has dried.

CHILD AND PET SAFETY

It's wonderful to be able to include indoor plants in our homes; however, some plants may pose a potential danger to our pets, children or also adults if they come into contact with the plant sap or the plant is ingested. The following list of plants is by no means a complete list of all the plants that may be poisonous to pets and children, so it's important to check with your veterinarian about the plants you have in your home and also keep plants out of the reach of inquisitive children. It's also a good idea to wear gloves and not to touch your eyes or face when handling indoor plants, to avoid contact with potentially irritating plant sap. Wash your hands well after handling indoor plants.

Use caution with the following plants:

- African mask plant (*Alocasia amazonica*)
- aloe vera (*Aloe barbadensis*)
- arrowhead plant (*Syngonium podophyllum*)
- Chinese evergreen (*Aglaonema* spp.)
- corn plant (*Dracaena fragrans*)
- croton (*Codiaeum variegatum*)
- devil's ivy (*Epipremnum aureum*)
- dragon tree (*Dracaena marginata*)
- dumb cane (*Dieffenbachia* spp.)
- English ivy (*Hedera helix*)
- fiddle leaf fig (*Ficus lyrata*)
- flamingo flower (*Anthurium scherzerianum*)
- heartleaf philodendron (*Philodendron scandens*)
- jade plant (*Crassula ovata*)
- Japanese aralia (*Fatsia japonica*)
- mother-in-law's tongue (*Sansevieria trifasciata*)
- never never plant (*Ctenanthe* spp.)
- peace lily (*Spathiphyllum wallisii*)
- philodendron (*Philodendron bipinnatifidum*)
- rex begonia (*Begonia rex-cultorum*)
- rubber plant (*Ficus elastica*)
- string of pearls (*Senecio rowleyanus*)
- Swiss cheese plant (*Monstera deliciosa*)
- umbrella tree (*Schefflera actinophylla*)
- weeping fig (*Ficus benjamina*)
- ZZ plant (*Zamioculcas zamiifolia*)

PROPAGATION

You can easily propagate many of your favourite indoor plants at home. Who doesn't want more plants for free! And it's so satisfying to see a new plant grow from just part of a plant. Plants can be propagated using three main methods: leaf cuttings, stem cuttings and division. Here are the basics for each method:

LEAF CUTTINGS

Plants like rex begonias, African violets, succulents and watermelon peperomia can be propagated via their leaves. Healthy leaves can be cut into sections, or entire leaves used to create new plants. Leaf cuttings work best when taken during the warmer months of the year, when the plant growth is at its fastest.

For rex begonias and watermelon peperomias, use a clean sharp knife to cut leaves into several wedges or simply cut the leaf in half horizontally. Each segment should have a vein or veins running through it. Dip the vein side of the wedge into some Yates Clonex Purple Hormone Rooting Gel and insert it gently, vein side down, into a pot or tray of moist Yates Seed Raising Mix and carefully firm the mix down around the leaf base. Keep the mix moist by regularly misting with water. You can also place the pot or tray inside a plastic bag (a sealable bag is ideal, three-quarters closed) to help retain moisture. Roots should grow from the leaf veins in a month or so and then the tiny plants can be planted into their own pots to grow.

For African violets, cut a leaf with a 2–3cm piece of stem attached. Dip the end of the stem into some Yates Clonex Purple Rooting Hormone Gel and then gently insert the stem end into a small pot of moist Yates Seed Raising Mix. Place a plastic bag over the pot to help keep in moisture. Mist the mix regularly with water. A baby African violet should grow from the base of the stem in a few months and can then be potted up into its own container.

For succulents like the jade plant, gently remove an entire leaf from the stem, let it dry out for a few days and then gently push the stem end into slightly moist cacti and succulent potting mix. Roots will form within a few months.

TOP LEFT: African violet leaf cutting
TOP RIGHT: Begonia leaf cutting
ABOVE: Succulent leaf propagation
RIGHT: Begonia propagation

STEM CUTTINGS

Stem cuttings involve taking a 10–15cm piece of stem that has several nodes on it (nodes are bumps along the stems where leaves emerge). Remove 75% of any foliage and then dip the cut end of the stem into Yates Clonex Purple Rooting Hormone Gel and gently insert that end into a pot of moist Yates Seed Raising mix and firm down gently around the cutting. Keep the mix moist by regularly misting with water. You can also place the pot in a plastic bag to assist moisture retention. Roots will develop from one or more of the nodes and a new plant will grow. Stem cuttings usually work best when taken during summer or early autumn when stems have matured slightly and are not new and soft. Plants like fiddle leaf fig, rubber plant, dumb cane, Swiss cheese plant, devil's ivy, corn plant, dragon tree, croton, hoya, baby rubber plant, philodendron, umbrella tree, zebra plant, arrowhead plant, flamingo flower, English ivy and waffle plant can be propagated with stem cuttings.

For plants like the dragon tree and corn plant that have woody stems, you can take 20cm-long pieces of stem (they don't have to have any leaves), dip the lower cut end into Yates Clonex Purple Hormone Rooting Gel (remember which end is the lower end!) and insert into moist seed raising mix. Roots will emerge from nodes along the stem.

You can also try placing stem cuttings in a vase or jar of water, where they can form roots. Some plants will develop roots quite quickly, which are easy to see if you're using a clear glass container. Once several good-sized roots have grown, the cutting can be gently planted into a pot filled with potting mix. Some cuttings will take a while to recover from this transition from water to potting mix and it's important to keep the potting mix moist during this initial establishment phase.

TOP: Stem cutting of peperomia
ABOVE: Aloe vera showing 'pups'

DIVISION

Some plants form clumps that can be divided up into smaller clumps. Plants such as cast iron plant, mother-in-law's tongue, peace lily, spider plant, peacock plant and Chinese evergreen are suitable for dividing. Once a plant has outgrown its current pot or has become congested with lots of roots and stems, remove the plant from the pot and carefully cut the clump into two or three sections using a sharp knife or a pair of secateurs. The aim is to retain as many roots and stems in each clump as possible. Plant the separate clumps into their own containers. Division is best done during the warmer months when the plant is actively growing. This will encourage faster recovery from being divided.

Succulents like zebra cactus and aloe vera can develop baby plants, called pups, around the mother plant, which can be removed once they have formed some of their own roots. Bromeliads can also be divided once they have developed pups, when they are around one third to half the size of the mother plant. These pups may not have any roots of their own; this is all right, as they slowly develop roots once they are potted into their own container.

On a general propagation note, please be aware that you can't propagate and sell plants that are protected by plant breeders' rights (which will be noted on plant tags).

TOP: Rooting cutting in water
ABOVE: Division

TOOL KIT FOR INDOOR PLANT GROWERS

- Watering can with a narrow spout – for accurate watering
- Plastic water spray bottle – for misting humidity-loving plants
- Gloves – to protect your hands from potting mix, tools and plant sap
- Dust mask – to avoid inhaling potting mix
- Sharp secateurs – for trimming and tidying stems and old flowers or taking cuttings
- Sharp knife – for taking leaf cuttings
- Small trowel – for handling potting mix
- Saucer of pebbles – for humidity-loving plants
- Supports, totems, trellises or stakes – for tall growing or climbing plants
- Plant fertiliser – for promoting healthy growth

GENERAL TROUBLE-SHOOTING

Each of the 50 plant profiles in this book contains advice about what conditions that plant likes, such as levels of light, humidity and watering. Sometimes plants will exhibit symptoms that indicate they aren't happy in their current location or with the care they're receiving. Some of the most common symptoms and causes include:

YELLOW LEAVES

- Overwatering – check moisture levels in the potting mix with your finger and adjust watering according to the plant's needs.
- Ageing leaves – yellow leaves can be a natural phenomenon as they mature and fall from the plant. They can be trimmed off if desired.
- Under feeding – pale foliage can indicate a lack of nutrients. Feed with a fast acting, complete liquid fertiliser.
- Too much light – some plants can pale if subjected to too much light. Move the plant to a slightly less well-lit position.
- Pests – check for mite or aphid infestations, which can cause leaves to mottle and yellow.
- Diseases – check foliage for signs of diseases like powdery mildew.
- Time to re-pot – if the plant has been in the same pot for several years, it may need to be re-potted into a slightly larger pot or its current potting mix may require refreshing.

BROWN LEAF TIPS

- Overwatering – check moisture levels in the potting mix with your finger and adjust watering according to the plant's needs.
- Direct sunlight – most indoor plants like bright but indirect light. Direct light can burn leaf tips. Move the plant to a position out of direct sunlight.
- Lack of humidity – during hot dry weather, humidity-loving plants can show browning of their leaf tips. Mist foliage with water and consider placing the pot on a water-filled saucer of pebbles, to help increase the humidity around the plant.
- Over feeding – over application of fertilisers can cause browning of leaf tips. Flush the potting mix with fresh water and reduce the frequency of feeding.

WILTING

- Underwatering – leaves can wilt if the plant is not receiving enough water. Check moisture levels in the potting mix with your finger and adjust watering according to the plant's needs.
- Waterlogged soil – plants growing in poorly drained potting mix or pots, or that are being overwatered, can exhibit drooping leaves, as their roots are starved of oxygen and may start to rot. Check moisture levels in the potting mix with your finger and adjust watering according to the plant's needs. Choose a pot or potting mix with improved drainage.
- Root rot – plants with root rot disease will often start to wilt, due to their inability to absorb sufficient moisture. Check moisture levels in the potting mix and adjust watering, choose a pot with improved drainage and apply a fungicide if required.

SCORCHED LEAVES

- Direct light – for most indoor plants, direct sunlight can damage the leaves. Move the plant to a more protected position.

LEGGY GROWTH

- Lack of sunlight – plants that don't receive their ideal amount of sunlight can start to grow long and lanky stems as they search for light. Move the plant into a more brightly lit spot.
- Incorrect feeding – can be caused by too much nitrogen, the nutrient that promotes green leaf and stem growth. Feed with a complete, balanced plant food.

LACK OF FLOWERS

- Under feeding – flowering plants need higher levels of the nutrient potassium to promote flowering. Feed with a potassium-enriched complete plant food, like Yates Thrive Roses & Flowers, to encourage flowers.
- Lack of light – some plants need bright light to promote flowers. Move the plant to a brightly lit spot to encourage flowers.

TOP RIGHT: This leaf has been scorched by direct sunlight.

BOTTOM RIGHT: Yellow leaves can be a sign that a plant is in trouble (see page 199)

REDUCED LEAF COLOUR

- Lack of light – plants with colourful or variegated foliage usually require more light than green foliage plants. Move plants to a more brightly lit position.

LEAF FALL

- Change in location – some plants do not like to be moved and will drop their leaves in response. Find their ideal location and try to leave them there.
- Exposed to change in environment – sudden exposure to draughts or air conditioning can shock plants. Move plants to a more protected position.

YATES PRODUCT GUIDE FOR INDOOR PLANTS:

- Yates Thrive All Purpose Liquid Plant Food
- Yates Thrive Roses & Flowers Liquid Plant Food
- Yates Thrive Orchid Liquid Plant Food
- Yates Thrive Houseplant Liquid Plant Food
- Yates Premium Potting Mix
- Yates Seed Raising Mix
- Yates Nature's Way Vegie & Herb Spray (Natrasoap)
- Yates Nature's Way Citrus & Ornamental Spray (Aust. only)
- Yates Nature's Way Organic Citrus, Vegie & Ornamental Spray (NZ only)
- Yates Nature's Way Natrasoap Vegie Insect Gun (NZ only)
- Yates Rose Gun
- Yates Fungus Gun
- Yates Liquid Copper Fungicide
- Yates Anti Rot Phosacid Systemic Fungicide (Aust. only)
- Yates Waterwise Soil Wetter
- Yates Clonex Purple Rooting Hormone Gel

REFERENCES:

For more details about the benefits of indoor plants to health and well-being, here are some interesting references:

www.sciencedirect.com/science/article/pii/S2211335516301401

en.wikipedia.org/wiki/NASA_Clean_Air_Study

www.plantlifebalance.com.au

www.uts.edu.au/sites/default/files/indoor_plant_brochure_2014.pdf

interiorplantscape.asn.au/wp-content/uploads/2016/04/Plants-in-the-classroom-can-Improve-Student-Performance-Report-2010.pdf

hortsci.ashspublications.org/content/44/5/1377

en.wikipedia.org/wiki/Crassulacean_acid_metabolism

INDEX

Page numbers in **bold** indicate a plant's main entry; page numbers in *italics* indicate a photograph

PHOTOGRAPH CREDITS

Page 3 Shutterstock/ Altin Osmana. 4 Shutterstock/ ananaline. 6 Shutterstock/ Jim Byrne Scotland. 8 Shutterstock/ Galiyah Assan. 9 Shutterstock/ 9Air. 10 Shutterstock/ CLICKMANIS. 13 Shutterstock/ Artazum. 14 Shutterstock/ Amilau. 15 iStock/ sapozhnik. 16 Shutterstock/ photographee.eu. 17 Shutterstock/ Enrika Samulionyte. 18 iStock/ GavinD. 19 Shutterstock/ Didecs. 20 Shutterstock/ Foto2rich. 21 Shutterstock/ Yuliya Yesina. 22 (top) Shutterstock/ Myimagine. 22 (bottom) Shutterstock/ Myimagine. 23 Shutterstock/ Jodie Johnson. 24 & 25 GAP Photos/ Friedrich Strauss. 26 Shutterstock/ Photographee.eu. 27 Andrea Johnson, HarperCollins Publishers. 28 Andrea Johnson, HarperCollins Publishers. 29 Shutterstock/ Wlad74. GAP Photos/ Visions. 31 GAP Photos/ Friedrich Strauss. 32 Shutterstock/ Olga Miltsova. 33 Shutterstock/ pfsa. 34 Shutterstock/ Shaiith. 35 (top) Shutterstock/ yougoigo. 35 (bottom) Shutterstock/ klevers. 36 Shutterstock/ KANOWA. 37 Shutterstock/ 0802. 38 Shutterstock/ dalton t. 40 (top left) Shutterstock/ Bozhena Melnyk. 40 (top right) Shutterstock/ 685628968. 40 (bottom left) Shutterstock/ Melica. 40 (bottom right) Shutterstock/ Naphat_Jorjee. 42 Shutterstock/ CLICKMANIS. 43 Shutterstock/ giedre vaitekune. 44 Shutterstock/ Irina Borsuchenko. 45 Shutterstock/ Kosobu. 46 Shutterstock/ Stanislav71. 47 Shutterstock/ Colette3. 48 Shutterstock/ thefoodphotographer. 49 Shutterstock/ Suchita Suphawilai. 50 (top) Shutterstock/ Screened. 50 (bottom) Shutterstock/ dgloris Marys. 51 Shutterstock/ HALCHYNSKA KSENIIA. 52 Shutterstock/ rattiya lamrod. 53 Shutterstock/ yurisyan. 54 Shutterstock/ Mirage_studio. 55 Shutterstock/ photopixel. 56 Shutterstock/ imnoon. 58 GAP Photos/ Visions. 61 Shutterstock/ Martin LAW. 62 Shutterstock/ haireena. 64 Shutterstock/ Photology1971. 67 GAP Photos/ Visions. 69 GAP Photos/ Visions. 71 & 72 GAP Photos/ Friedrich Strauss. 74 Shutterstock/ Sarun T. 76 Shutterstock/ InfoFlowersPlants. 78 GAP Photos/ Visions. 81 Shutterstock/ Patrycja Nowak. 83 GAP Photos/ Friedrich Strauss. 84 Shutterstock/ GoodMood Photo. 87 Shutterstock/ TanaSSS. 88 Shutterstock/ Anastacie. 90 Shutterstock/ Sergey Clocikov. 92 Shutterstock/ GoodMood Photo. 95 Shutterstock/ Shelsea Forward. 97 Shutterstock/ InfoFlowersPlants. 98 Shutterstock/ touristgirl. 100 GAP Photos/ Howard Rice. 103 GAP Photos/ Howard Rice. 105 GAP Photos/ Visions. 106 Shutterstock/ grintan. 108 GAP Photos/ Clive Nichols/ Clare Matthews. 111 Shutterstock/ Suko-Image. 113 GAP Photos/ Visions. 114 Shutterstock/ ncristian. 116 Shutterstock/ merindadesigns. 118 Shutterstock/ grasslifeisgood. 121 GAP Photos/ Friedrich Strauss. 122 Shutterstock/ Oleg Samoylov. 124 GAP Photos/ Friedrich Strauss. 126 Shutterstock/ Shatsh. 129 GAP Photos/ Howard Rice. 130 Shutterstock/ Alessio Rinaldi. 132 Universal Images Group North America LLC/ DeAgostini Picture Library/ Alamy Stock Photo. 135 GAP Photos/ Friedrich Strauss. 137 Shutterstock/ fneum. 138 Shutterstock/ Bozhena Melnyk. 140 Shutterstock/ MariaNikiforova. 142 GAP Photos/ Friedrich Strauss. 145 Alamy Stock Photo/Photoshot License/ Avalon. 146 Angie Thomas. 148 Shutterstock/ tdee photo cm. 151 GAP Photos/ Visions. 152 Shutterstock/ PhotoLohi. 154 Shutterstock/ yevgeniy11. 157 Shutterstock/ Photo and Vector. 158 Shutterstock/ Alena Brozova. 160 (top left) Shutterstock/ Vitali Michkou. 160 (top right) Shutterstock/ vasara. 160 (bottom left) Yates. 160 (bottom right) Shutterstock/ sanddebeautheil. 163 (top) Shutterstock/ Julia Caro. 163 (bottom) Shutterstock/ Shebeko. 164 Shutterstock/ photographee.eu. 167 (top) Shutterstock/ funkyfrogstock. 167 (bottom) Andrea Johnson, HCP. 169: Shutterstock/ hedgehog 94. 171 Shutterstock/ imnoom. 173 Shutterstock/ Taras Garkusha. 175 Shutterstock/ JRP Studio. 177 Shutterstock/ Photographee.eu. 178 (left) NPK diagram is trademark of Yates. 178 (right) Angie Thomas. 179 Shutterstock/ TatianaMara. 181 Shutterstock/ polarpx. 183 (left) Shutterstock/ tetiana_u. 183 (right) cha_cha. 185 (top left) Shutterstock/ Henrik Larsson. 185 (top right) Shutterstock/ cha_cha. 185 (centre left) Shutterstock/ Tomasz Klejdysz. 185 (centre right) Shutterstock/ Photo Fun. 185 (bottom left) Angie Thomas. 185 (bottom right) Shutterstock/ chanchai loyjiw. 187 (top left) Shutterstock/ Ishtvan Rishko. 187 (top right) Angie Thomas. 187 (bottom left) GAP Photos/ Geoff Kidd. 187 (bottom right) Shutterstock/ stocksuwat. 188 (top left) Shutterstock/ Stanislav71. 188 (top right) GAP Photos/ Geoff Kidd. 188 (bottom left) Angie Thomas. 190 Shutterstock/ Okssi. 192 Shutterstock/ Audrey Lohkamp. 193 (top) Shutterstock/ Nick Mayorov. 193 (bottom) Shutterstock/ Anna Nahabed. 195 (top left) Gap Photos/ Paul Debois. 195 (top right) Gap Photos/ John Swithinbank. 195 (bottom left) Shutterstock/ Jacob Henwood. 195 (bottom right) Gap Photos/ Jonathan Buckley. 196 (top) Gap Photos/ Friedrich Strauss. 196 (bottom) Shutterstock/ S_Sukporn. 197 (top) Shutterstock/ Pong Wira. 197 (bottom) Gap Photos/ Friedrich Strauss. 198 Shutterstock/ Agnes Kantaruk. 201 (top) Angie Thomas. 203 (bottom) Shutterstock/ mdbildes.

AUTHOR'S NOTE

To all the current and future indoor plant devotees, may your life be overflowing with fabulous greenery.

Gardening and indoor plants have brought an immense sense of happiness and well-being into my life and it's fantastic to be able to share a passion for plants with my fellow gardening-addicted Yates team members. I would like to sincerely thank Tammy Huynh, Matthew Gerakios, Steph Robson, Eric Bharucha and Kylie Grigg for their research and writing contributions in this book and their tireless enthusiasm and dedication to all things leafy.

To my family, thank you for your patience and support while I was writing this book, and to HarperCollins, thank you for your encouragement and help in bringing the book together.

HarperCollins*Publishers*

First published in Australia in 2018
by HarperCollins*Publishers* Australia Pty Limited
ABN 36 009 913 517
harpercollins.com.au

Copyright © DuluxGroup (Australia) Pty Ltd and Angie Thomas 2018
Yates ® is a registered trademark of DuluxGroup (Australia) Pty Ltd

The right of Angie Thomas to be identified as the author of this work has been asserted by her in accordance with the *Copyright Amendment (Moral Rights) Act 2000*.

This work is copyright. Apart from any use as permitted under the *Copyright Act 1968*, no part may be reproduced, copied, scanned, stored in a retrieval system, recorded, or transmitted, in any form or by any means, without the prior written permission of the publisher.

HarperCollins*Publishers*

Level 13, 201 Elizabeth Street, Sydney NSW 2000, Australia
Unit D1, 63 Apollo Drive, Rosedale, Auckland 0632, New Zealand

A catalogue record for this book is available
from the National Library of Australia

ISBN 978 1 4607 5734 5

Cover and internal design by HarperCollins Design
Cover photo © Eve Wilson / thedesignfiles.net
Back cover image by shutterstock.com
Colour reproduction by Graphic Print Group, South Australia
Printed and bound in China by RR Donnelley on 157gsm matt art

8 7 6 5   19 20 21 22